Handbook of Demographics for Marketing and Advertising

Handbook of Demographics for Marketing and Advertising

Sources and Trends on the U.S. Consumer

William Lazer
Florida Atlantic University

Lexington Books
D.C. Heath and Company/Lexington, Massachusetts/Toronto

Library of Congress Cataloging-in-Publication Data

Lazer, William.
Handbook of demographics for marketing and advertising.

Includes index.
1. Consumers—United States. I. Title.
HC110.C6L39 1987 305.6'0973 86-46440
ISBN 0-669-16013-X (alk. paper)

Published simultaneously in Canada
Printed in the United States of America
International Standard Book Number: 0-669-16013-X
Library of Congress Catalog Card Number: 86-46440

The paper used in this publication meets the minimum requirements of American National Standard for Information Sciences—Permanence of Paper for Printed Library Materials, ANSI Z39.48-1984.

87 88 89 90 8 7 6 5 4 3 2 1

To Joyce, the eminent scholar's partner

Contents

Foreword

Perhaps ever since Plato observed that "You can't step twice into the same river," the world has recognized change if not its significance. This book is about change and its significance.

All business functions ought to be concerned with change, but this observation especially applies to marketing. In compelling ways marketing should establish and lead the other functions comprising a business. For marketing to do so requires that it sense and seize demographic changes, the wellspring of so many other changes. Professor Lazer meets this important test. Pulse-point chapters concern themselves with income, wealth, and affluence; employment trends; geographic shifts; minorities; working women; household composition trends; and the aging population, among other topics. Individually and collectively, these are the forces that drive (and sometimes deter) markets and associated marketing strategies. Although knowledge of these shifting market dynamics won't guarantee marketing success, to be ignorant of them is to court disaster. By focusing on what the marketer needs to know about the trending consumer market, Lazer provides us with a most useful context for analyzing present and anticipating future markets and strategies aimed at profitably participating in those markets.

There seem to me to be too many people still relying on stereotypical ideas and profiles about what constitutes the marketplace. Too often the conventional wisdom readily endorses accepted but questionable marketing stereotypes, such as the elderly, the babyboomers, yuppies, and the like. Mere use of these terms implies group homogeneity that attentive researchers and scholars know simply doesn't exist. In this regard, Lazer, the scholar, examines within-category differences. He defines, describes trends, draws contrasts on both longitudinal and cross-sectional bases, and analyzes and suggests relationships. These are valuable contributions because they prod the reader beyond the obvious. Thereby, useful learning results.

Likely the readers will discover their own favored chapters and treatments. Following are a few of mine:

> Chapter 1 establishes the connections between changing demographics and their marketing impacts. Although these connections should be obvious to adept marketers, Professor Lazer reminds us anew of their significance, and he does so early in a tone-setting way.
>
> Chapter 2 contains worthwhile insights into segmentation niches that income and wealth trends portend. Personally, I urge marketers to pay increasing attention to wealth beyond—but not at the expense of—income. Wealth reflects income, but income does not necessarily reflect wealth. The author's perspective and treatment of wealth can aid such a focus.
>
> Chapter 5 offers the serious student quite useful initial perspectives on the nature and importance of market segmentation associated with race and ethnic characteristics of our population. Because our population is increasingly heterogeneous, such clear and cogent distinctions are commensurately important for marketers to understand and to reflect.
>
> Chapter 8 is a jewel because it challenges the still all-too-prevalent stereotypical thinking and undifferentiated treatment of the older population by marketers. Comparatively and compellingly, Professor Lazer brings to the surface lifestyle differences and their marketing implications.

I hope these examples will induce readers to discover their own insights.

This book's composition and style also deserve recognition. Professor Lazer conveys his subject with a varied and balanced style: numeric blended with nonnumeric evidence; description complemented by analysis; tables and graphs effectively interspersed in text; and past data melded into projected data. Together with a consistently readable writing style, these qualities provide this work with an appealing format and form. Some prospective readers probably regard these as trivial advantages, undeserving of formal review, evaluation, and mention. I disagree. Too often important content in a book is seriously underconveyed because other authors lack Dr. Lazer's orientation toward the reader.

Although I have a professional disagreement with separating advertising from marketing in the book's title (advertising is *part* of marketing), this decision is someone else's domain. However, I find the "handbook" notion in the book's title to be an arresting concept. Virtually all of the handbooks I know about are tomes, ponderous to behold and sometimes to use. In contrast, this slim version is a handbook in the true sense of the term—that is, "a book capable of being *conveniently* carried as a ready reference manual." The book concurrently meets the handbook test of "a concise reference book covering a particular subject or field of knowledge." The book is true to its subtitle, *Sources and Trends on the U.S. Consumer.* Supplying sources and trends are other valuable (and rightly expected) obligations of a handbook. In short, this is a handbook that doesn't look like a handbook. It invites handbook-type use as well as cover-to-cover reading. This is unusual. My judgment is that teachers, students, and practitioners alike will benefit from this enlightened approach. In a world of so-called niche marketing, this rare approach doesn't fill a niche but rather creates a niche. Other authors and publishers might do well to take note.

—John G. Keane, Director
U.S. Bureau of the Census

Preface

This book is based on the use of census statistics for over three decades, the pursuit of numerous projects for businesses, and hundreds of presentations before academic and business audiences in North America and abroad. The foundations of the book were established in the early 1970s, when I was asked by a large U.S. manufacturer of consumer durables to assemble a group of distinguished behavioral scientists to undertake a project concerned with future consumer life-styles and product–market opportunities. That experience kindled a continuing and growing interest in two areas of concern to business: demographic developments and futures research. This interest was nurtured further by the many insights gained while serving as a member, and later as chairman, of the Census Advisory Committee (Marketing).

In the early 1970s I addressed executive development programs on the impact of changing demographics on marketplace activities. Those assignments led to numerous presentations for companies, professional associations, universities, business classes, trade groups, and public audiences. These contacts spawned research papers in a variety of publications in academic and business journals, as well as in the general press. They spurred further investigations into the implications of our changing demographics and life-styles.

These pursuits fostered increased understanding of the relationships between a good grasp of demographics and the effective performance of such important business activities as strategic planning, understanding consumer wants and needs, new product development, company and product positioning, and strategic decision making. The lack of attention given to critical demographic factors and their likely impact on business in marketing and other business administration courses was underscored. It also became painfully clear that relatively few business executives, particularly those at the top levels, were conversant with the major demographic and lifestyle changes that were continuously reshaping present and future opportunities for their own companies.

Discussions with colleagues confirmed that these voids existed in both the academic and business worlds and that there was the lack of an easy reference source on "marketing demographics." This was substantiated by the fact that professors, researchers, and executives have contacted me continuously about using slides and materials that I have developed on demographics. Many requested comments on materials that they prepared for planning and decision-making purposes. Several suggested that a book be published dealing with changes in income, population, and related life-style factors that would affect future markets. Academicians indicated that such a book would serve as a useful reference and as collateral reading in such courses as consumer behavior, principles of marketing, marketing management, marketing strategy, product development, entrepreneurship, marketing research, and various management courses.

In the process of writing this book, I became even more aware of the caveat that population statistics and socioeconomic data make for rather dry reading. When masses of data are presented to business and academic audiences, regardless of their relevance, attention wanes. A "ho-hum" reception usually accompanies such unexpressed questions as "Who really cares?" and "So what?" Although appropriate answers might well be "You should!" or "It could make a great difference to you, your understanding of future opportunities, and performance on the job!" or "It could greatly benefit your institution and its effectiveness!" nevertheless, statistical figures and tables remain boring.

This book provides a ready reference for selected information about changing demographics and lifestyles and seeks to make them more interesting, meaningful, and relevant for decision makers. It is designed to bring the information to life for professional audiences by focusing on the future and developing some of the likely implications of the data for business. Hopefully, it will whet the appetites of readers so that they will pursue selected areas of interest in greater depth. References for future analysis are included at the end of the chapters.

A careful selection of socioeconomic data has been made, with many of the usual caveats, footnotes, and discussion of statistical methodologies eliminated. An overall portrait of selected dimensions of present U.S. consumers, along with projections for the future, is offered. The book focuses on some of the more important developments of the immediate past, longer-range trends, and discussions of what such trends are likely to mean for future business opportunities.

Choices have been made about the information to include, and perhaps more importantly, about what to exclude. Undoubtedly, important data have been ignored. But interested readers can readily follow up and pursue their particular areas of interest in depth, using the array of informative publications from government sources, particularly from the insightful and valuable publications of the Bureau of the Census.

This book is organized into two sections. Part I focuses on changing market dimensions and part II deals with socioeconomic dynamics. The four chapters in part I are concerned with population dynamics, income and wealth, employment trends, and geographic shifts and spatial factors. They deal with many of the fundamental structural elements that govern and reshape markets.

Part II considers important socioeconomic factors that will have great impact on how U.S. consumers will live and the purchases they will make, factors that will shape and fashion market opportunities. Included are chapters dealing with the American Mosaic, working women, households and families, mature consumers, and the new consumer. The last chapter, unlike the other chapters, is not heavily rooted in statistical data but relies on observations, insights, and conjectures. It is designed to be thought provoking; the ideas are open to challenge.

This book has five main objectives:

1. To provide a ready and convenient reference to some of the major demographic, income, and lifestyle trends that are shaping U.S. markets.

2. To indicate the vast array of government data and information that is pertinent and useful, particularly from the U.S. Bureau of the Census.

3. To highlight some of the significant demographic changes and implications, and how they shape business opportunities and practices.

4. To stimulate readers to pursue in-depth analysis of data in areas of particular interest to them, and to suggest likely data sources.

5. To encourage thought about likely implications of future demographic, income, and life-style developments, particularly with references to readers' own interests.

If modest progress can be made in achieving several of these goals, then the efforts of the many people involved in preparing the materials will have been worthwhile. The book presents one person's observations only, and other observers may disagree completely, or at least have different perspectives, and choose to emphasize different developments. But that is the nature of any serious consideration and interpretation of demographic data.

I am deeply indebted to several members of the U.S. Bureau of the Census who read the manuscript very carefully and critically. They checked for errors, updated data, raised theoretical issues, and extended both the breadth and depth of the analysis. As a result, the book was improved and the presentation was strengthened. Those who participated and shared their comments so freely are Arthur Cresce, Statistician, Population Division; Diane DeAre, Statistician, Population Division; Carmen D. DeNavas, Statistician, Population Division; Edna Le Paisano, Acting Chief, Racial Statistics Branch, Population Division; John F. Long, Chief, Population Projections Branch, Population Division; Thomas J. Palumbo, Supervisory Statistician, Population Division; Steve W. Rawlings, Statistician, Population Division; Paul Ryscavage, Labor Economist, Population Division; Cynthia Taeuber, Special Assistant for Selected Populations, Population Division; Edward Welniak, Survey Statistician, Population Division; James R. Wetzel, Chief, Center for Demographic Studies; and Arno I. Winard, Supervisory Statistician, Population Division. My sincerest thanks and deepest appreciation is offered to them.

I am grateful to a respected friend and colleague, Dr. Jack Keane, Director, Bureau of the Census, for his generous sharing of insights, advice, and guidance throughout the years. His thoughtfulness in writing a foreword for the book is greatly appreciated. As a leader in the area of strategic marketing planning and the management of change he has long been interested in the market implications of demographic and lifestyle changes.

Many other people contributed to this book in a variety of ways. Dean Gary A. Luing of the College of Business and Public Administration at Florida Atlantic University has continuously supported my research and writing activities and encouraged the pursuit of academic endeavours. Areta Cummings generously lent her superb secretarial and artistic skills over an extended period of time. The interest of Caroline McCarley, editor at Lexington Books, was instrumental in bringing the book to completion. Several graduate assistants over the decades at Michigan State University worked with census data and helped prepare charts and tables. Eleanor Boyles, a librarian's librarian at Michigan State University, was a continuous source of assistance. The secretarial staff at Florida Atlantic University, particularly Margaret Murphy, Jean Sorenson, Gloria Thompson, and Patty Singer, assisted so willingly in the preparation of materials for the manuscript, as did Maureen Rafferty. To all who were so helpful, both recognized contributors and those who have been inadvertently overlooked, I extend my heartfelt thanks.

This book is dedicated to my dear wife Joyce, a treasured partner and companion in all of life's journeys, a constant source of inspiration and support throughout more than thirty years of married life. She makes all things possible.

As with most books, inevitable errors and glitches are bound to occur. I extend sincere apologies well ahead of time and accept full responsibility for them while expressing the hope that they will not be numerous or too troublesome.

Part I

Changing Market Dimensions

1
Population Dynamics: The Changing People Base

Changing Markets

The new demographics indicate how dramatically the face of the U.S. market has changed since the mid-1960s. Our markets are no longer dominated by babies, teenagers, or young adults. Future projections indicate even greater shifts away from the younger segments. The face of the U.S. consumer is rapidly becoming more weathered and wrinkled as we witness the continuing aging and greying of an increasingly affluent United States.

Ours is an era in which some age categories will realize the most marked and sharp demographic changes in our history. Some age categories will decrease significantly; others will expand. The result will be increasing pressure on businesses to adjust their market focus.

Though the general thrust of major demographic developments since the mid-1960s has been quite evident, companies nevertheless have often been caught off guard. Not only did they tend to ignore shifting demographic structures, but the 1980 census also brought a few surprises. An experienced marketing executive pointed out a situation that exists in too many companies. After listening carefully to a presentation on changing demographics and future trends the executive noted, "Our company has been paying ever-increasing attention to the declining markets, while ignoring those that are emerging."

Many marketing activities reflect these population changes:

> The use of older, grey-haired, more natural looking models in advertisements, replacing the exclusive emphasis on youth and beauty queens.
>
> The development of skin creams and lotions to deter the effects of aging, and regenerate and restore aging skin.
>
> The cultivation of markets for adult food and drinks, the emphasis on health foods, vitamins, exercise regimens, and plastic surgery, and other products dedicated to maintaining a more youthful appearance.
>
> The great increase in health services marketing.

Despite the aging population, youth is revered in the U.S. society and age and seniority are not as respected as they are among other cultures.

In *Managing in Turbulent Times,* Drucker noted that the demographic underpinnings of U.S. markets are now veering in new directions that will create new opportunities, new markets, new business patterns, and the need for new social action. The population dynamics "will challenge widely held beliefs regarding the structure and segmentation of consumer markets. . . . [They] will stand on their heads some of the most cherished beliefs and habits of business" (Drucker 1980).

This chapter discusses such basic factors as future population growth, birthrates, and changing age distributions. We shall examine their likely impact on product and service opportunities, and particularly what will happen as a result of population shifts and the evolving topology of markets between 1985 and the turn of the century.

Population Growth

Markets are people with the money and willingness to buy. Businesses, both those concerned with consumer and industrial products and services, should be very interested in population growth, overall and by age segments. Population growth is of course a function of both net immigration and net internal growth, and the excess of births over deaths.

The United States is now feeling the impact of increasing pressures from people around the world who wish to immigrate. The pressures are so great that legislative bills have been advanced dealing with the limitation of immigration. Legal immigration for several decades has remained in the 400,000 to 425,000 per annum range. Illegal immigration, however, in the form of undocumented aliens, has risen to unprecedented heights. Exact figures are impossible to obtain, but guesses are that the illegal immigration for the decade of the 1970s alone totaled between 3 and 5 million. And it seems reasonable to believe that, because of the relentless pressures, they will total at least that amount in the 1980s and 1990s. This is indicative of the continuing impact that people from other cultures will have on U.S. markets.

Immigration not only adds to the total population, but it affects our tastes, life-styles, methods of business operations, and employment and market opportunities. The surface impact is evidenced by such ethnic items as pizzas, bagels, tacos, croissants, and European and Asian clothing styles that have been integrated into the U.S. way of life. The deeper impact is felt in the form of changes in our families, homes, religious institutions, laws, and communities.

Births and Population Growth

Shifting from immigration to population growth from within, birth expectations in the United States remain relatively low. The birth rate is not expected to exceed 2.1 births per woman. If that rate is maintained for several decades it will result in zero population growth. At present, the average number of lifetime births for women aged 18–44 is approximately 2,023 per 1,000 women. The current rate for all women is just over 1.8, below the replacement level. It seems that the birthrate will continue to be relatively low.

In general, women seem to expect about 2 children over their lifetimes—one of each gender—a sort of "matched set." In reality, however, among women aged 18–24, there were only 1.99 births per woman, a picture that has remained relatively unchanged since

Table 1–1
U.S. Population: 1970–2000
(in thousands)

Age	*1970*	*1980*	*1990*	*2000*
Under 5	17,154	16,348	19,200	17,264
5–14	40,745	34,942	35,375	38,277
15–19	19,070	21,168	16,957	18,950
20–24	16,371	21,318	18,567	17,126
25–34	24,907	37,082	43,506	36,387
35–44	23,088	25,634	37,845	43,718
45–54	23,220	22,800	25,391	37,094
55–64	18,590	21,703	21,090	23,779
65–74	12,436	15,580	18,054	17,693
75 +	7,630	9,040	13,745	17,343
Total	203,211	226,545	249,731	267,990
Median Age	30.6	31.3	33.0	36.3

Source: Bureau of the Census 1984d.

1978. Low birthrates are here to stay for the near future, and the family of 6, 8, 10, or 12 children of the 1920s, 1930s, and 1940s is a thing of the past. We shall have smaller sized, more portable families as a result.

At the start of 1987 the total U.S. population was estimated to be about 242 million. As is shown in table 1–1, about 23 million people, or slightly less than the population of Canada, was added to the United States over the decade of the 1970s. A similar increase is expected over the decade of the 1980s, but that, of course, is on a larger population base. Thus, the growth rate is slower and it will likely continue to be so. Population growth will be reduced in the 1990s to an expected 18 million, a 22-percent decrease, resulting in a total population of about 268 million by the year 2000. This is well below the 300 million figure commonly projected in the 1950s. We are becoming a slow-population-growth country.

Beyond the year 2000, total population growth is expected to

Table 1–2
U.S. Population Growth, Middle Series Estimates: 1900–2020
(in thousands)

Year	*Number*
1900	76,303
1930	122,775
1940	131,669
1950	150,697
1960	179,323
1970	203,302
1980	226,505
1990	249,731
2000	267,997
2010	283,141
2020	296,339

Source: Bureau of the Census 1984d.

increase, but at a decreasing rate to about 16 million for the decade 2000 to 2010 and to only 13 million between 2010 and 2020. This is shown in table 1–2. Both the actual and percentage growth in population are traced from the first census taken in 1790 to 1980 in figure 1–1, highlighting a persistent downward trend. Most of the growth over the next century will occur in the next 50 years.

Slow Growth

The U.S. population will grow more slowly from now until the middle of the next century, when it is virtually expected to cease growing. By then we shall likely reach zero population growth. The annual percentage change in population from 1950 to 1960, which was in the 1.7 range, declined to the 1.05 range from 1970 to 1980. It is only expected to be in the 0.92 range between 1980 and 1990, in the 0.7 range from 1990 to 2000, and to continue its decline for 100 years to 2080. From 2030 to 2080 the population is projected

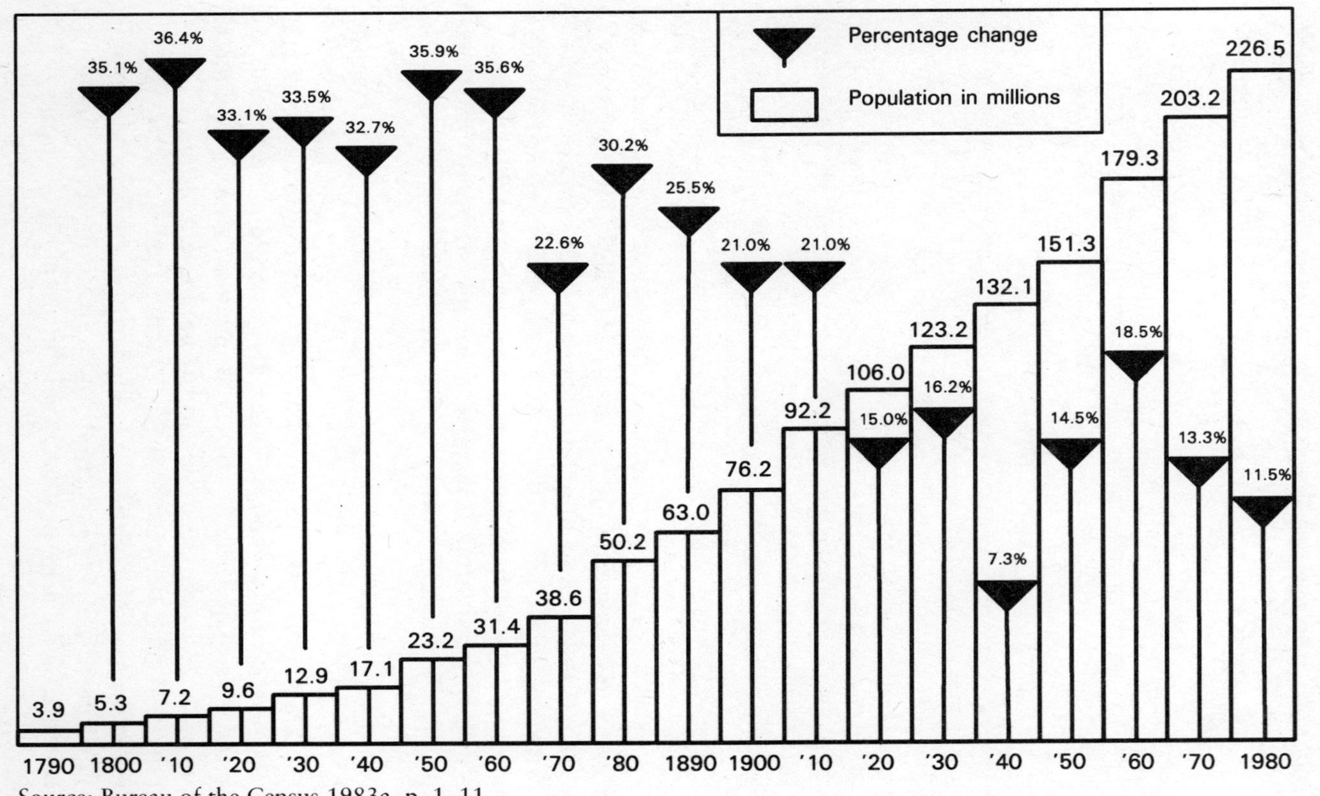

Source: Bureau of the Census 1983a, p. 1–11.

Figure 1–1. *Total Population and Percentage Change from Preceding Census for the United States: 1790–1980*

to increase by less than 6 million people—a radical transformation. All the demographic evidence indicates that businesses that have been propelled by growing populations in the past (and they number a great many) will have to set their plans and strategies to gear them to much lower population growth. The United States will truly become a slow-population-growth nation. The projections for 2030–80 that total population growth will be less than 6 million present a far different picture from our immediate past, a picture that will radically transform business approaches and strategies. For, rather than expanding population pulling inefficient businesses along, we shall require far more efficient businesses designed to cultivate slow-population-growth and no-population-growth markets. Productivity, efficiency and competition will become keys to management in the future.

The addition of a baby to a childless household, as marketers will realize, has a profound effect on how life is lived, on household activities and routines, and on purchasing decisions and patterns. The actual number of live births powers the demand for a variety of products and services, such as housing, automobiles, clothing, baby food, pharmaceuticals, apparel, toys, sporting equipment, medical care, and the like. A major force behind the high economic growth years, the 1960s ("the soaring '60s") was the high birthrate and large number of live births.

The baby boom occurred right after the end of World War II through 1964. The birthrate rose, and the greatest number of live births occurred between 1954 and 1964 when births averaged more than 4 million, hitting a peak of 4.4 million in 1957. The first half of the 1960s realized an average of 4 million live births per year, a figure that we have not matched since. The so-called baby boomers, therefore, were 21–30 years old in 1985.

As is shown in table 1–3, in the 1970s the number of live births tapered off and fell. Currently, it is picking up a little and has increased every year since 1975. It is expected that before the 1990s we will once again approach 4 million live births but then the total will likely tend to decline and level off by 1995. Birth expectations and the birthrate remain relatively low because women now expect to have about 2.1 children over their lifetimes.

Table 1–3
Live Births
(in thousands)

Year	*Births*
1940	2,570
1950	3,645
1957	4,400
1960	4,307
1970	3,725
1975	3,144
1980	3,413
1985	3,700
1995	3,600[a]

Source: Bureau of the Census 1985b.
[a]Author's estimate.

First Born

An interesting shift is occurring in the proportion of first births among families, and this has a resounding effect on markets. Traditionally, about 25 percent of the births were first births, but by 1982 they increased to 38 percent. Because consumers spend far more on the first birth than on any succeeding child (some estimates are over twice as much), the market impact is expected to be more substantial than the overall total of births suggest. When a baby first enters a family the proud parents are willing to spend freely and generously. Succeeding children, however, receive far fewer considerations and are the recipients of "the hand-me-downs." Also, the addition of a baby renders some products obsolete such as a sports car, the bachelor pad, small metropolitan apartments, coin laundries, and similar singles items.

There has also been a change in the age of birthing. Women are now postponing babies and having them later in life. Previously, women felt that 30 was the automatic cutoff age for births. If no child was born by the time a woman reached 30, it was deemed "now or never." In the 1980s, however, a growing proportion of first children were born to women in the early and late 30s. More women are delaying child birth until their 30s. Women 30–34 years old showed an increase in births from 60 to 69 per 1,000 women between 1980 and 1983, while no other age group had a significant change. Medical advances can handle the complications feared previously.

Women having their babies later in life include the better educated and better paid. These families are often able to provide a much better home environment. With smaller-sized families, they are able to devote more attention to their children. This augurs well for the demand for baby-related products and services, including not only the usual baby food, clothing, furniture, and pharmaceuticals, but such items as day-care centers, preschool nurseries, flexible work time, and products promoting the automation of household chores. Those items that effectively accommodate mothers, particularly working mothers, will be in great demand.

Changing Age Structures

Some idea of the population dynamics at work can be gained by investigating both the actual and expected total and proportionate changes in the age composition of the population from 1970 to the year 2000. Referring back to table 1–1 (which gives the age breakdown of the U.S. population in 1970 and 1980 along with estimates to the year 2000), the aging and greying of the population is evident as the median age shifts markedly from 31.3 years in 1980 to an estimated 36.3 years in the year 2000. This is a striking increase and highlights the decades of the growing importance of 35–44, 45–55, and 65-and-over age categories. The 35-and-over age groups, particularly those 65 and over, will grow. The 25-and-under categories will show declines or very limited growth from 1990 to the year 2000, but the decades of the middle-agers and senior citizens are rapidly emerging.

The market changes between 1970 and 1980 among age categories are highlighted in figure 1–2. The percentage decline of the very young, the increase of the 25–34 group until 1990, and the growth of every over-50 category is marked. The 1970s were truly a decade powered by the young marrieds with their young families—the 25–34-year-olds. These are people interested in establish-

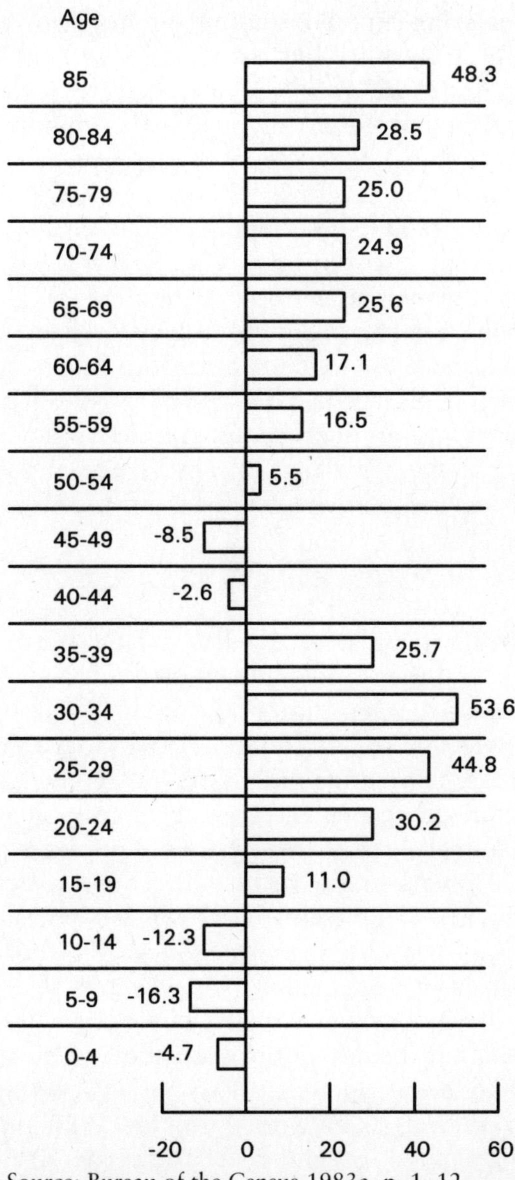

Source: Bureau of the Census 1983a, p. 1–12.

Figure 1–2. *Percentage Change by Age: 1970–80*

ing themselves in their homes, communities, families, and jobs. Generally, they were rather conservative and not as rebellious in their outlook, contrary to what some social observers and media stories during the 1970s would have led us to believe. Ours has been a fairly stable rather than a rebellious society. The traditional values have been maintained. It is not so much a return to the previous values that is occurring. Rather, the United States in general never left those values—the rest of the 25–34-year-olds supported them.

Population Shifts

The actual population shifts by decades from 1980 to 2000 are given in table 1–1; the percentage changes are shown in table 1–4. Proportionately, in the 1980s the 35–44 segment (the early middle-agers) will grow by 46 percent. The senior citizens (the 65-and-over group), will increase, and the 75-and-over category will almost double. The 25–34 segment, the largest segment in 1980, will peak in 1990 and then decline a little. We are rapidly become a middle-aged society and the 35–54 age groups will be a key market focus to the turn of the century.

As figure 1–2 shows on a percentage basis that the 55-and-over group, particularly the elder categories, realized substantial growth between 1970 and 1980. The very old, the 85-and-over group, grew by 48.3 percent, the 80–84 group by 28.5 percent, and the 70–74 group by 24.9 percent. But, in total, they are still a small market.

In 1980 the 65-and-over segment totaled 25,554,000 and is projected to grow by about 40 percent to 35,036,000 by 2000. The 75–84 sector totaled 7,727,000; the 85-and-over group was a surprising 2,240,000. These are currently neglected markets and we shall examine them in detail in chapter 8.

The ratio of the working-age population (those 18–64 years of age) to the retirement age population will soon begin an unprecedented decline. In 1982, the United States had 5.3 people of working age for every person 65 or older. The ratio will be 4.7 in 2000, 2.7 in 2030, and 2.4 in 2080.

The proportionate changes for the next two decades, from 1980–90, and 1990–2000, are summarized in table 1–4. The most striking shifts are the 48-percent growth in the 35–44 age group

Table 1–4
U.S. Population: Percentage Change 1980–90 and 1990–2000

Age	*1980–90*	*1990–2000*
Under 5	17.0	−10.0
5–14	1.0	8.0
15–19	−20.0	12.0
20–24	−13.0	−8.0
25–34	17.0	−16.0
35–44	48.0	16.0
45–54	11.0	46.0
55–64	−0.03	13.0
65–74	0.16	−0.02
75+	0.52	26.0

Source: Bureau of the Census 1985a.

from 1980 to 1990, and the 46-percent growth in the 45–54 age group from 1990 to 2000. Similarly, the decreases in the 15–24 group in the 1980s, and the under-5 and 20–34 groups in the 1990s, coupled with 26 percent growth in the 75-and-over groups, represent marked changes from the immediate past.

Figure 1–3 shows the striking changes in the distribution of our population by age and sex from 1982 to the year 2080. In 1982, the median age reached 30.6 years, an all-time high, but never again is it projected to be so young. From 36.3 years in the year 2000, it is expected to grow to 42.8 years in 2080. The 1982 population pyramid is concentrated in the bottom portions, reflecting a relatively young population. By the year 2000 there is quite a change and by 2030 and 2080 the concentration in the upper age categories clearly reflects the aging and greying of the United States.

Life Expectancy

Over the century, the life expectancy in the United States has jumped strikingly from an average of 49 years in 1900 to 70 years in 1954, and an amazing 74 years in 1981. This represents a 50 percent increase in life expectancy. Estimates are that in 2000 it will

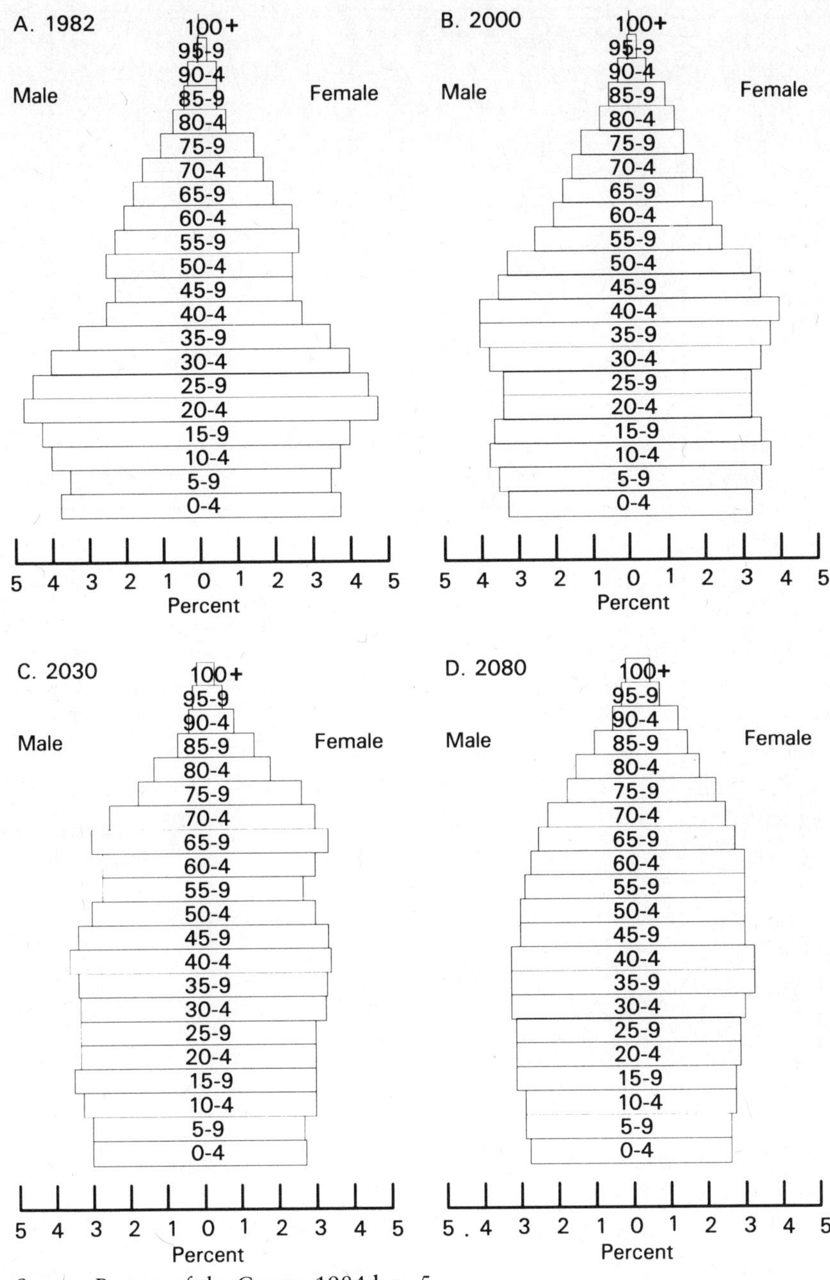

Source: Bureau of the Census 1984d, p. 5.

Figure 1–3. *Percentage Distribution of the U.S. Population, by Age and Sex*

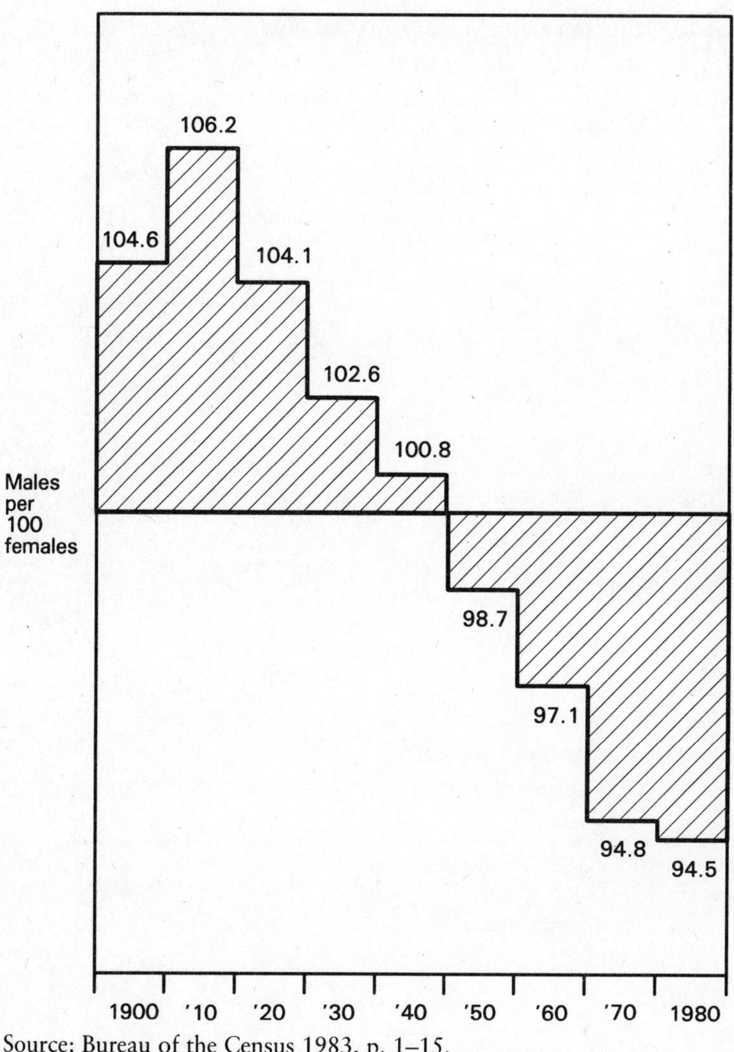

Source: Bureau of the Census 1983, p. 1–15.

Figure 1–4. *Sex Ratio: 1900–80*

be 76.7 years and by 2030 the average life expectancy will be almost 80 years.

The life expectancy of women now exceeds that of men by about 8 years. The dramatic impact of this fact on the sex ratio, males per 100 females, is shown in figure 1–4. Also, the life expectancy for males who reached age 65 in 1978 was another 14 years;

Table 1–5
Market Focus by Decades

Decade	*Market Focus*
1950 and 1960	Babies
1960 and 1970	Teenagers
1970 and 1980	Young adults and young marrieds
1980 and 1990	Early middle-agers
1990 and 2000	Late middle-agers
2000 +	Mature consumers

for females it was 18.4 years. This portends an increase in the elderly of our society, particularly elderly women, with the increasing demand for both public and private goods such as health-care centers, nursing homes, hospitals, medical and pharmaceutical products, and related services. As the population ages, older males become a scarce resource.

Market Focus

The general market focus of each of the preceding decades is characterized in table 1–5. Thus, the 1950s, overlapping with the early 1960s, were the baby-boom years. The 1960s and early 1970s saw the teenage market thrive. The 1970s and 1980s marked the years of young adults and the 1980s, overlapping with the 1990s, will be the decade of the middle-agers—first, the younger middle-agers and then the older middle-agers. They represent the future focus which, of course, will be followed by the mature consumers to be discussed in chapter 8.

These trends suggest the decline and rise of demand for different kinds of products and services associated with each stage of life. Table 1–6 breaks down market opportunities by life-cycle trends.

Summary

Demographic shifts are radically reshaping marketing opportunities. General population thrusts such as the aging and greying of our population, or the movement of people to the West and South have been quite clear and to an extent, predictable. Yet, the implicit

Table 1–6
Biological Life Cycle and Consumption

Stages in Biological Life Cycle	*Consumption Life Cycle*	*Market Opportunities*
Infancy	Bodily maintenance	Baby foods; infants' wear and furniture; pharmaceuticals; toys
Childhood	Adjustment to daily living; school; social adjustment	Child care; educational services; household recreational equipment; toys; video games
Adolescence	Occupational training; adult role playing	Fast foods; clothing; electronic products; automobiles; job-related training; adult entertainment
Pair bonding	Marriage and household formation; acquisition	Furniture; houses and apartments; household goods; appliances; life and property insurance; repair services
Reproduction	Full nest; acquisition; replace purchases	Child care; baby-sitting; legal and financial services; baby foods; furniture and equipment
Middle life	Empty nest; divorce	Recreation; travel; retirement services; trust and investment services; health foods; clothing; plastic surgery; cosmetics; luxury goods
Aging	Maturity; elderly; retirement	Medical services; retirement services and communities; gifts; burial services; health foods; leisure; hospitals; pharmaceuticals; skin cream; cosmetics; recreation; mobile homes

Source: Fisk 1982.

opportunities they suggest have been ignored by a large proportion of the U.S. business community. Population dynamics are forcing a reevaluation of the structure of markets.

Our population growth is governed by immigration and the excess of births over deaths. Immigration pressures have been increasing, particularly from illegal immigrants, and this affects our lifestyles, labor force, employment opportunities, families, homes, and communities. Although current low birthrates are anticipated for the immediate future, projections are that our population will grow by about 23 million in this decade and by some 18 million in the 1990s. Beyond the year 2000 total population growth is projected to slow to 16 million and then 13 million in the first two decades of the next century. Ours will likely be a slow-population-growth country adding perhaps 6 million people in the 50 years from 2030 to 2080. Businesses will be challenged to establish slow-population-growth marketing strategies.

The baby-boom years from the end of World War II through 1964 heralded a burst of live births, which peaked at 4.4 million in 1957. It has tapered off but is now increasing gradually and is expected to reach 4 million once again before 1990.

The proportion of first born is increasing and has almost reached 40 percent. The addition of a baby to a family greatly influences consumption patterns. Women are having children later in life and an increasing proportion of first born are to women over 30.

The median age of our population is shifting markedly from 31.3 years in 1980 to an estimated 36.3 years in 2000. The growing importance of the 35–54-year-old age group and the 65-and-over group is eclipsing the young marrieds—the 25–34-year-olds who dominated the markets of the 1970s. We are rapidly becoming a middle-aged society with an average life expectancy approaching 77 years by the year 2000.

From 1980 to 2000 the overall market focus is shifting to the early and late middle-agers. After 2000 the focus will become the mature consumers. The result is continuously shifting market opportunities for products and services.

References

Bureau of the Census. 1983a. *1980 Census of Population: General Population Characteristics*. Vol. 1.

———. 1983b. *1980 Census of Population: General Social and Economic Characteristics*. Vol. 1.

———. 1984a. *Estimates of the Population of the United States by Age, Sex, and Race: 1980 to 1983*. Series P-25, no. 949.

———. 1984b. *Fertility of American Women: June 1982*. Series P-20, no. 387.

———. 1984c. *Fertility of American Women: June 1983, Population Characteristics*. Series P-20, no. 386.

———. 1984D. *Projections of the Population of the United States by Age, Sex, and Race: 1983 to 2080*. Series P-25, no. 952.

———. 1985a. *Estimates of the Population of the United States by Age, Sex, and Race: 1980 to 1990*. Series P-25, no. 965.

———. 1985b. *Statistical Abstract of the United States, 1986*. 106th ed.

Drucker, Peter F. 1980. *Managing in Turbulent Times*. New York: Harper and Row.

Fisk, George. 1982. "Marketing Implications of an Aging Workforce." *The Collegiate Forum* (Fall):18–19.

2
Income, Wealth, and Affluence

An Overview

Income distribution traditionally took on the shape of a triangle, with relatively few wealthy persons at the top and most of us at the bottom. But the income triangle is becoming more rectangular in shape both as an increasing number of persons and households become more affluent, earning incomes of over $50,000 over the next decade, and as the poorer households move steadily up the income ladder. It is a dynamic scene and the overriding conclusion is that the next decade will mark a steady, persistent, and substantial increase among the more affluent segments of our economy.

It is not just people, but people with money who are of interest to marketers. Despite this interest, data on income distributions are not as readily available as they are for demographic factors. Also, income data can be misleading as indicators of capacity to buy for they ignore wealth, taxes, changing tastes, and other assets.

The census regularly publishes reports on money income of individuals and families in the United States. The results are derived from a sample of over 60,000 households. In 1983, median family income reached $24,580, an increase of 1.6 percent from 1982, the first increase in real family income (allowing for inflation) since 1979 (Bureau of the Census 1984). Per capita income increased to $12,700 at the same time the poverty rate remained around 15 percent (Bureau of the Census 1984).

Several caveats should be borne in mind when using income data. Census data refer to regularly received money income only. Excluded are transfer payments such as Social Security income and welfare payments; all noncash payments and benefits such as Medicare and food stamps; and gifts, wealth, assets, and unreported income. Thus, some consumers who are classified as poor can in reality be asset wealthy. Also, marketers are very interested in discretionary income and know well that pretax income may not be available for expenditures.

Family Income and Affluence

Tables 2–1 and 2–2 deal with 1983 family incomes as reported by the census. Table 2–1 details the percentage distribution of family incomes, in current dollars, for 1970, 1975, 1977, 1980, and 1983. Continuous growth occurs in both the mean and median incomes (although that is not the case for constant dollars). There is a de-

Table 2–1
Family Income, 1970–83: Percentage Distribution by Income Categories
(1983 dollars)

Total Money Income	*1983*	*1980*	*1975*	*1970*
Number of Families (thousands)	61,997	60,309	56,245	52,227
Under $2,500	2.2	2.1	3.4	6.6
$2,500–$4,999	3.5	4.1	8.7	12.5
$5,000–$7,499	5.0	6.2	10.5	15.0
$7,500–$9,999	5.2	6.5	10.7	16.7
$10,000–$12,499	6.1	7.3	11.3	15.8
$12,500–$14,999	5.5	6.9	11.0	11.0
$15,000–$19,999	11.8	14.0	18.8	13.1
$20,000–$24,999	11.5	13.7	11.6	4.6
$25,000–$34,999	19.5	19.8	9.5	3.0
$35,000–$49,999	17.0	12.8	3.2	1.1
$50,000+	12.6	6.7	1.4	0.5
Total	100.0	100.0	100.0	100.0
Median income	$24,580	$21,023	$13,719	$ 9,867
Mean income	$28,638	$23,974	$15,546	$11,106

Source: Bureau of the Census 1984, p. 8.

Table 2–2
Income of Families and Unrelated Individuals: 1983

Total Money Income	*15–24*	*25–34*	*35–44*	*45–54*	*55–64*	*65+*	*Total*
Under $1,000	1,166	2,545	1,614	1,075	1,273	2,220	9,893
$10,000–$19,999	1,119	3,608	2,634	1,605	1,995	3,589	14,549
$20,000–$24,999	426	1,964	1,542	927	1,128	1,123	7,110
$25,000–$34,999	364	3,286	3,017	2,125	1,955	1,343	12,089
$35,000–$49,999	158	2,316	2,963	2,403	1,845	854	10,539
$50,000–$74,999	23	759	1,666	1,663	1,169	387	5,667
$75,000+	—	157	627	721	480	166	2,151
Total	3,258	14,632	14,062	10,519	9,843	9,682	61,997
Median income	$13,841	$22,776	$28,944	$32,592	$27,407	$16,862	$24,580

Source: Bureau of the Census 1984.

crease in the number and proportion of under $20,000 families and a significant increase in the more affluent families, particularly the $50,000-and-over families.

Table 2–2 breaks down families by 1983 income and age of the householder. The concentration of more affluent families can be seen in the 35–54-year-old categories. As is to be expected, the 45–54 households have significantly higher median incomes than any other one group and income decreases substantially in the 65-and-over group, reflecting retirement.

The increase in U.S. affluence is underscored by facts such as these:

The 30 richest people in the United States own $3.68 billion.

In 1982, 206 people in the United States had incomes of at least a million dollars a year (*Forbes* 1983).

In 1982, there were 15 billionaires in the United States (*U.S. News and World Report* 1983).

Compared with many other industrialized countries, such as Japan, we are a nation with great income variations: the wealthy, a very large middle class, and the poor. In 1984, for example, 55 executives had salaries and bonuses alone of over $1 million (in 1984 dollars), and many more made over $500,000. Yet over 15 percent of the U.S. population lives below the poverty level. One in 5 adults in 1982 were classified as affluent, living in households with over $40,000 (in 1982 dollars), more than three times the well-to-do in 1978 (*Wall Street Journal* 1983). And the average income in these affluent households was estimated at $72,900, compared with $18,300 in nonaffluent homes. Affluent households represented 14 percent of the 80.7 million households and accounted for 37 percent of personal income.

The following are some census findings about 1983 income as compared with 1982 (Bureau of the Census 1984):

Although 1983 median income of white families ($25,760) increased 1.4 percent over 1982, the median for black families ($14,510) and Spanish families ($16,960) did not increase.

Table 2–3
Family Median Incomes: 1983
(in 1983 dollars)

All families	$24,580
White families	25,760
Black families	14,510
Hispanic families	16,960
Families with college-educated householder	40,520
Married-couple families	27,290
Married-couple families with working wife	32,110
Married-couple families without working wife	21,890
Female householder, no husband present	11,790

Source: Bureau of the Census 1984.

Families with a college-educated householder, as compared with noncollege-educated householders, had significantly higher median incomes—$40,520—an increase of 2.6 percent over 1982.

Married-couple families had median incomes of $25,290, an increase of 1.6 percent.

Families with a female householder, no husband present, had a median income of only $11,790.

Real median income of men increased to $14,630, up 1.6 percent; that of women was $6,320, up 4.0 percent.

Table 2–3 highlights some of the facts about median family income in 1983.

Discretionary Income

Marketers are very interested in discretionary income, "income in excess of that for necessaries, income over which consumers can exercise discretion in making purchases." But such data are quite scarce. The most notable study results from a joint effort of the Conference Board and the Bureau of the Census, using 1981 income data. Discretionary income in that report is defined "as the amount of money that would permit a family to maintain a standard of living higher than the average of that of similar families" (Linden, Green & Coder no date, p. 7). In determining similar families, the size, ages, and place of residence are considered.

Over 25 million households, about 31 percent, had discretionary income totaling almost $200 billion. They had 55 percent of pretax income, or about 51 percent of the after-tax income.

About 28 percent of the after-tax income of these households was discretionary income. There has been an ongoing escalation of households with money available for luxury expenditures. As a result, luxury spending has been rising rapidly. Estimates are that in 1990 total discretionary income in 1980 dollars will be about $325 billion—an increase of almost two-thirds (Linden, Green & Coder no date, p. 8).

The demographic, social, and economic characteristics of discretionary income households include the following:

Mean incomes are 75 percent higher than the national average.

One-third of the discretionary income households have incomes of $40,000 and over.

The 40–64 age bracket are 39 percent of all households and have 53 percent of spendable discretionary income.

The 65-and-over age group accounts for 17 percent of all spendable discretionary income.

Per-capita discretionary income of all households increases after age 60.

The under-30 homes have little discretionary income.

Discretionary income households are largely two- (or more) income households accounting for 60 percent of all discretionary income households and 63 percent of the money.

Average discretionary income is much higher where only the husband works.

Discretionary income households include a well-above-average number of working wives.

Discretionary income households are well-educated households, including one-half of all homes with a head who earned a college degree; these households account for 43 percent of the discretionary buying power.

The professional and managerial class are disproportionately large among discretionary income households and have half of the spendable discretionary dollar.

In general, the geographic distribution of discretionary income parallels that of the population.

Average household income of suburban communities is substantially higher than that of central cities, whereas per-capita income is higher in the central cities than it is in the suburbs.

Black households have both smaller average after-tax incomes and per-capita income than white households.

Blacks have about 13 percent of all households and 5.5 percent of all discretionary income.

Hispanics have 4.7 percent of all households and 2.2 percent of all discretionary income.

Discretionary income is significantly higher among home owners than renters.

Table 2–4 summarizes some of the above information on estimates of spendable discretionary income (SDI). Households with incomes of $50,000 and over are but 17 percent of the total, but have 46 percent of the aggregate SDI. The $40,000-and-over households (34 percent of households) have almost two-thirds of the SDI. The data highlight the widespread availability of SDI among households overall, as well as a proportionately higher amount in the $40,000-and-over households.

Poverty and Affluence

Regardless of increasing affluence, the poverty status of consumers must also be considered. In 1983, where the poverty threshold for

Table 2–4
Households with Discretionary Income: 1980

Income	*Number of Households (thousands)*	*% of Households with Discretionary Income*	*Spendable Discretionary Income*	
			Aggregate ($ Billion)	*Average*
Under $15,000	1,740	6.9%	$ 3.4	$ 1,940
$15,000–$19,999	1,678	6.6	4.8	2,874
$20,000–$24,999	2,747	10.9	9.3	3,402
$25,000–$29,999	3,564	14.1	13.1	3,684
$30,000–$34,999	3,877	15.3	18.7	4,829
$35,000–$39,999	3,119	12.3	19.7	6,303
$40,000–$49,999	4,178	16.5	35.8	8,563
$50,000–$74,999	3,338	13.2	52.9	15,841
$75,000+	1,051	4.2	35.6	33,888
Total	25,292	100.0	193.3	

Source: Linden, Green & Coder no date, p. 19.

a family of four was $10,178, 35.3 million people were reported to be living in poverty compared with 34.4 million (15 percent of the population) in 1982. The increase is the result of a growth in unemployment in families maintained by women with no husbands, and in households with unrelated individuals (Bureau of the Census 1984). This census report includes these findings:

> Estimates of the poverty level populations are significantly lower if the value of noncash benefits is included. Depending on what is included, 1982 estimates range from 22.9 million (10 percent) to 31.4 million (13.7 percent).
>
> Black households (35.6 percent) and Spanish households (29.9 percent) had significantly higher poverty rates than white households (12.0 percent). There were no changes from 1982.
>
> The overall poverty rate among families was 13.6 percent; for married-couple families it was only 8.9 percent, but for female householders without husbands it was 40.6 percent, and for unrelated individuals it was 23.1 percent.

Geographically, the poverty rate for households was highest in the South (18.1 percent), followed by the West (14.1 percent), the North Central region (13.3 percent), and the Northeast (13.0 percent).

A Look to the Future

Marketers, strategic planners, and other company executives are interested in what the future income pictures may be like. Such data are not readily available and prognosticators can be sure of one fact—their predictions will invariably be wrong. Nevertheless, we shall make some predictions about likely future household incomes bearing the usual caveats in mind.

The following analysis of future income refers to census income data as defined previously. The data are based on census income projections and are derived by applying an average annual real income increase of 1.5 percent for the most part and a rate of 2.0 percent where indicated (Bureau of the Census 1981). They have been selected as reasonably conservative estimates of likely future average increases. They are considerably lower than the 3.3 percent and 3.0 percent of the 1950s and 1960s, and somewhat lower than the current rates. However, they are higher than the 0.7 percent average growth rate of the oil shock decade of the 1970s. Household distributions by income classes are also obtained from census projections (Bureau of the Census 1981). A computer program was used to interpolate and smooth the data.

Will these projections approach reality? That is a difficult question to answer, for some recent statistics suggest that many in the United States are now struggling just to keep what they have. Some workers have taken pay cuts and given up benefits, such as cost-of-living adjustments, just to keep their jobs. Average hourly earnings have not grown in the 1980s, and in 1984 median household income was $26,433, about 6 percent below 1973 in real dollars. The possibility of the occurrence of downward mobility exists (*New York Times* 1986). To maintain their family incomes the bulk of the households now have multiple wage earners, and whether this reflects an increase in family incomes and living standards has been questioned.

Household Incomes

In 1995, the number of U.S. households with incomes under $25,000 will be about the same as was the case in 1980. But for the first time the number of households with incomes above $25,000 is expected to be equally as large. And the new affluence will not be limited to the managerial and professional classes, nor to those in a few chosen careers, or even to households in specific age or educational brackets. Rather, it will be "democratic affluence" cutting across all types of households and extending well beyond what businesses traditionally considered markets for high-priced, high-quality products and services.

The number of households earning $35,000 or more in 1980 dollars will increase rapidly between 1980 and 1990. The $50,000-and-over category will increase by 87 percent, and the $35,000-and-over category by 62 percent, as is seen in table 2–5. Between 1980 and 1995, 24.5 million households will be added. The $50,000-and-over income sector will increase by roughly 8 million households (a 150-percent increase), and will make up one third of the increase in households. The $35,000-and-over households will experience an increase of about 14.9 million (a 99-percent increase), to make up 60 percent of the 1980–95 increase.

Although households with incomes of $25,000 and under will increase by 5.6 million, they hardly signify affluence, but neither need they represent only underprivileged classes. A large proportion of them are singles' households that, in all likelihood, have lighter fixed expenditure burdens and a higher proportion of discretionary income than would most husband-and-wife households with similar incomes. Some indication of this may be gleaned from the findings that singles' households with incomes of $25,000 have over twice as much per-capita discretionary income as do three-person households earning over $40,000 per year (Linden, Green & Coder no date, p. 27).

From the data on income projections we can conclude that:

1. Overall, the future household income picture to 1995 is one of increasing and mass affluence.

Table 2–5
Growing Household Affluence: 1980–95
(1.5% growth rate; households in thousands)

	1980		*1990*		*1995*	
Income	*Number of Households*	*% of Households*	*Number of Households*	*% of Households*	*Number of Households*	*% of Households*
Under $10,000	20,563	25.80	22,286	23.03	22,423	21.52
$10,000–$19,999	21,021	26.37	23,135	23.90	23,603	22.65
$20,000–$24,999	9,419	11.82	10,098	10.43	10,587	10.16
$25,000–$34,999	13,749	17.25	17,110	17.68	17,775	17.06
$35,000–$49,999	9,737	12.22	14,412	14.89	16,731	16.06
$50,000 +	5,215	6.54	9,752	10.08	13,075	12.55
Total	79,704	100.00	96,793	100.00	104,194	100.00

Note: Data are based on the author's projections, using the methodology described in Chapter 2. Percentages may not sum to 100 percent due to rounding.

2. Most of the household growth will occur among the more affluent households, notably the $35,000–$49,999 and $50,000-and-over categories.
3. The total number of under-$25,000 households will grow very slowly and actually show a proportionate decrease.
4. The lower-income households, the $10,000–$24,999 categories, have a heavy concentration of singles' households that could represent substantial discretionary purchase power and a market base reflecting more of the "good life" than that income bracket tends to suggest.

Middle-aged Households

Table 2–6 and 2–7 present breakdowns of the number of households by age group and by income. Data are given for the young marrieds (the 24–34-year-olds), the early middle-agers (the 35–44-year olds), and the late middle-agers (the 45–54-year-olds). In chapter 8 (on mature consumers) we shall deal with incomes of households 55 and over.

The growth of middle-aged households will eclipse that of the young marrieds that dominated the 1970s. From 1980 to 1995 the early middle-agers (the 35–44-year category) will add about 97 million households, while the late middle-agers (the 45–54-year-olds) will add another 51 million households. The 24–34-year-old households will increase by only 41 million households at the same time, about 30 percent of the middle-aged total.

The data point up a shift in concentration from the 25–34-year-old households in the $10,000–$19,999 and $25,000–$34,999 income classes in 1980, to the $35,000–$49,999 and $50,000-and-over 35–44-year-olds in 1995. Very rapid growth occurs in the $35,000-and-over 45–54-year-old households.

Table 2–8 summarizes shifts in household income by age of the householders. For instance, among the 35–44 households, 9.64 percent made $50,000 and over in 1980, but by 1995 the total is projected to be 17.20 percent.

Increasing affluence among middle-aged households is highlighted. Substantial changes occur among 35–54-year-old house-

Table 2–6
Affluent Middle-aged Households: 1980
(as multiples of 100,000 households)

	Age of Householder		
Income	*25–34*	*35–44*	*45–54*
Under $10,000	29	19	17
$10,000–$19,999	57	31	24
$20,000–$24,999	30	20	14
$25,000–$34,999	40	33	27
$35,000–$49,999	22	26	25
$50,000+	6	14	17
Total	184	143	124

Note: Data are based on the author's projections, using the methodology described in Chapter 2. Percentages may not sum to 100 percent due to rounding.

Table 2–7
Affluent Middle-aged Households: 1995
(as multiples of 100,000 households)

	Age of Householder		
Income	*25–34*	*35–44*	*45–54*
Under $10,000	31	28	20
$10,000–$19,999	55	41	28
$20,000–$24,999	31	25	15
$25,000–$34,999	50	51	31
$35,000–$49,999	39	54	39
$50,000+	19	41	42
Total	225	240	175

Note: Data are based on the author's projections, using the methodology described in Chapter 2. Percentages may not sum to 100 percent due to rounding.

Table 2–8
The Shift to Household Affluence: 1980 and 1995
(as percentage of households)

	Age of Householder					
	25–34		*35–44*		*45–54*	
Income	*1980*	*1995*	*1980*	*1995*	*1980*	*1995*
Under $10,000	15.64	13.98	13.05	11.46	13.64	11.55
$10,000–$19,999	30.85	24.50	21.55	17.19	19.67	15.91
$20,000–$24,999	16.13	13.73	14.21	10.39	11.21	8.67
$25,000–$34,999	22.04	22.19	23.33	21.40	21.44	17.72
$35,000–$49,999	11.80	17.31	18.22	22.35	20.18	22.22
$50,000+	3.54	8.30	9.64	17.20	13.87	23.94
Total households (in thousands)	18,315	22,477	14,239	24,063	12,366	17,420

Note: Data are based on the author's projections, using the methodology described in Chapter 2. Percentages may not sum to 100 percent due to rounding.

holds in the $35,000-and-over income category. The largest single segment among them shifts from the $10,000–$19,999 households in 1980 to the $35,000–$49,999 bracket in 1995, followed by the $50,000-and-over households.

The 45–54-year-old group, the late middle-agers, marks a period when households on the average earn their highest income. As might be expected, the $50,000-and-over households will comprise the largest single income segment by 1995. And the $35,000-and-over households account for over 46 percent of the older middle-aged category. This is a period when the children are usually grown, educated, and living on their own so that the late middle-agers tend to feel freer to spend on themselves, live their own lives, and seek their own enjoyment.

Superaffluent Households

Marketers have always regarded husband–wife households as important purchasing units, and regardless of high divorce rates, they currently comprise the majority of U.S. households and, as already

Table 2–9
Husband–Wife Households: The Superaffluents, 1980–95
(1.5% growth rate; households in thousands)

	1980		*1990*		*1995*	
Income	*Households*	*%*	*Households*	*%*	*Households*	*%*
Under $10,000	5,660	11.73	4,716	8.89	4,134	7.53
$10,000–$19,999	13,721	24.30	10,463	19.72	9,590	17.58
$20,000–$24,999	6,690	13.87	5,865	11.05	5,517	10.12
$25,000–$34,999	11,093	22.99	11,981	22.57	11,295	20.71
$35,000–$49,999	8,457	17.53	11,750	22.14	13,062	23.95
$50,000 +	4,624	9.58	8,296	15.63	10,938	20.06
Total	48,245	100.00	53,076	100.00	54,536	100.00

Note: Data are based on the author's projections, using the methodology described in Chapter 2. Percentages may not sum to 100 percent due to rounding.

noted, will continue to do so. There will be significant shifts among husband–wife households to superaffluence in 1995, to households with incomes of $50,000-and-over in 1980 dollars. These households, regardless of their social class standing, will control a large proportion of our discretionary income and afford very affluent living standards.

Husband–wife household income reflects the proportion of working wives, which is highest among the upper income brackets. Table 2–9 shows that though the total number of husband–wife households will grow by over 6 million in the 1980–95 interval, surprisingly, the $50,000-and-over households will increase by about the same amount. And, although they make up one of the smaller income segments in 1980, by 1995 the $50,000-and-over bracket will become one of the largest sectors, almost 11 million households, about 20 percent of all husband–wife households. The next highest bracket, the $35,000–$49,999 category, will increase by about 4.6 million units, while the under-$35,000 households will show a steady decline. The affluent categories, the $35,000-and-over, will account for about 44 percent of the all husband–wife households.

The data suggest three major conclusions. First, mass affluence will become prevalent among husband–wife households with the proportion of $35,000-and-over households increasing from about 27 percent of the total in 1980 to almost 45 percent by 1995.

Second, there will be remarkable growth among the superaffluent husband–wife households, as almost 11 million of them will be in the $50,000-and-over segment. The widespread affordability of luxurious life-styles suggests extensive demand for high-quality products and services. Also, superaffluent consumers tend to be more discerning, demanding, eclectic, and cosmopolitan in their tastes, and bring a wider variety of products and life-styles into their homes.

Third, with the expected continuing decrease in the average size of families from about 3.25 persons in 1980 to 2.97 in 1995, members of husband–wife households will realize significant per-capita income gains. Household members will not only have more money to spend, but will likely become more independent, feel less fettered socially and economically, and freer to indulge themselves. Superaffluence will bring with it more confident consumers seeking to realize themselves and satisfy their particular needs; consumers will be able to express their individuality, uniqueness, and personalities in their purchases. They are less likely to feel pressured by the accepted tastes of the masses and more likely to seek self-expression and give greater emphasis to unique products and services, tailored to their needs and desires. They will be able to afford the luxury of making individual statements via their possessions, to indulge themselves in their purchases, and to feel more confident in doing so.

Husband–Wife Households

Tables 2–10, 2–11, and 2–12 highlight the striking movement up the income ladder, both absolutely and proportionately, among middle-aged husband–wife households between 1980 and 1995. As in the previous tables, the data assume a 1.5 percent annual income growth rate.

In 1980, the 25–34-year-olds made up the largest concentration of husband–wife households; the largest single income segment was the $25,000–$34,999 category, followed by the $10,000–$19,999

Table 2–10
Middle-aged Husband–Wife Households: 1980
(in multiples of 100,000 households)

	Age of Householder		
Income	*25–34*	*35–44*	*45–54*
Under $10,000	8	5	5
$10,000–$19,999	29	17	13
$20,000–$24,999	22	15	10
$25,000–$34,999	33	28	22
$35,000–$49,999	18	23	23
$50,000+	5	12	16
Total	115	101	88

Note: Data are based on the author's projections, using the methodology described in Chapter 2. Percentages may not sum to 100 percent due to rounding.

Table 2–11
Middle-aged Husband–Wife Households: 1995
(in multiples of 100,000 households)

	Age of Householder		
Income	*25–34*	*35–44*	*45–54*
Under $10,000	4	5	4
$10,000–$19,999	15	15	11
$20,000–$24,999	13	14	8
$25,000–$34,999	29	34	21
$35,000–$49,999	27	44	32
$50,000+	13	35	37
Total	102	146	113

Note: Data are based on the author's projections, using the methodology described in Chapter 2. Percentages may not sum to 100 percent due to rounding.

Table 2–12
Shifts in Affluence among Husband–Wife Household in Percentages: 1980 and 1995
(as percentage of households)

Household Income Category	*Age of Householder*					
	Young Marrieds (25–34)		*Early Middle-agers (35–44)*		*Late Middle-agers (45–54)*	
	1980	*1995*	*1980*	*1995*	*1980*	*1995*
Superaffluent ($50,000+)	4.51	12.69	12.20	24.04	17.94	32.59
Affluent ($35,000–$49,999)	15.82	26.91	23.19	30.30	25.40	28.29
Moderate income ($25,000–$34,999)	28.58	28.57	27.80	23.04	24.94	18.22
Poorer households (Under $25,000)	51.09	31.82	36.97	22.62	31.72	20.90
Total households (in thousands)	11,476	10,188	10,081	14,557	8,844	11,341

Note: Data are based on the author's projections, using the methodology described in Chapter 2. Percentages may not sum to 100 percent due to rounding.

group. By 1995, however, these young married households are eclipsed in numbers by both the early and late middle-aged households, which account for 72 percent of all husband–wife households. And the largest age–income segment is the 35–44 households with incomes of $35,000–$49,999 followed by the $50,000-and-over bracket. Among the late middle-aged households, the $50,000-and-over category (the superaffluents) rank first, followed by the affluent $35,000–$49,999 households.

The widespread, increasing affluence among middle-aged husband and wife households is clearly shown in table 2–12, where income categories are arranged on the basis of relative degree of affluence. The categories are superaffluents (households with incomes of $50,000 and over); affluents (households earning $35,000–$49,999); moderate households (incomes of $25,000–

$34,999); and the poorer households (those in the $25,000-and-under bracket). These household categories are further classified by age groups: young married (25–34); early middle-agers (35–44); and late middle-agers (45–54). Though the categories are somewhat arbitrary and ignore important factors other than income, such as family size and number of dependents, they are nevertheless indicative of the shifts within and among categories.

There will be a marked increase in the proportion of superaffluent and affluent households among all the age groups, particularly the early and late middle-agers. The middle-aged superaffluents will almost double over the period, accounting for about one-fourth and one-third of the 35–44-year-old and 45–54-year-old households, respectively. And about 55 percent of the early middle-aged households and 60 percent of the late middle-aged households in 1995 will at least meet the criterion of affluence, an amazing trend. Also, the moderate-income households will realize gains, while the poorer households decrease significantly both absolutely and proportionately.

The statements previously made about widespread, increasing affluence among all middle-aged households are even more pertinent to husband–wife household segments. For they truly represent a transition to mass affluence, great concentrations of discretionary purchasing power, and portend the most lucrative market segments.

The 1990s will be the decade of affluent and superaffluent middle-aged husband–wife households, and marketers would do well to keep their wants and needs clearly in focus. Middle-aged husbands and wives have the characteristics of being interested in their families, homes, communities, acquisitions, and indeed, the symbols portrayed by their purchases. They will come to expect, and indeed, will be able to afford "the best," which is often correlated with that which costs the most money. At the same time, a life-style of affluence, luxury, and aesthetic material acquisitions will be accompanied by greater attention to cultural and quality-of-life considerations. For husband–wife middle-aged households the future will, indeed, be that of a more graceful style of life and one of increasing self-indulgence.

With affluence comes leisure. Superaffluent consumers will be

Table 2–13
Estimates of Consumer Expenditures

Category	*% of 1941 Expenditures*	*% of 1980 Expenditures*
Food and beverages	23.7	18.1
Alcohol	5.2	2.6
Clothing	13.0	7.4
Housing	12.9	16.3
Household operation	14.7	13.7
Medical care	4.1	9.9
Personal business	4.2	5.4
Transportation	10.6	14.5
Recreation	5.2	6.4
Other	6.4	5.7
Total personal spending	$125 billion	$2,957 billion

Source: Bureau of Labor Statistics 1983.

able to indulge in leisure pursuits such as travel, recreation, sporting, and entertainment events. But leisure need not mean time with which to do nothing, for this time will likely be programmed leisure. In fact, there will probably be increasing competition for the consumers' expenditure of time. Consumers will be faced with a larger number of affordable, desirable, expenditure options and a decreasing amount of time with which to enjoy their material gains—a poverty of time.

Consumer Expenditures

We conclude this chapter with two tables dealing with consumer expenditures. The first, table 2–13, notes trends in the proportion of expenditures by categories of products and services for 1941 and 1980. The second, table 2–14, deals with consumer expenditures by age of the householder in 1980.

As compared with 1941, consumers in 1980 spent a significantly smaller proportion on food and beverages, and only about one-half as much on alcohol and clothing. However, proportionate

Table 2–14
Consumer Spending Patterns, by Age of Householder: 1980

Category	*Under 25*	*25–34*	*35–44*	*45–54*	*55–64*	*65 and Older*
Food at home	27.5%	32.5%	36.8%	33.1%	34.6%	37.5%
Food away from home	20.5	18.2	17.4	16.3	14.0	12.1
Alcoholic beverages	9.1	5.6	5.0	5.5	4.3	3.3
Tobacco products	4.2	2.8	2.6	3.0	2.8	2.2
Personal care	3.6	3.6	3.8	4.1	4.2	4.4
Nonprescription drugs	1.1	1.2	1.2	1.6	2.0	2.9
Housekeeping supplies	3.3	4.0	4.4	4.1	4.5	4.3
Energy supplies	30.7	32.1	31.3	32.3	33.5	33.2

Source: Bureau of Labor Statistics 1983.

expenditures on medical care more than doubled and transportation increased by almost 40 percent.

When the age factor is considered, proportionate food expenditures at home increase with age, while those away from home decrease. Expenditures on tobacco and alcohol are lower; those on nonprescription drugs are significantly higher, and those on personal care increase.

Summary

The income triangle is changing shape as more individuals and households move up the income ladder. Through 1995 we shall see a persistent and substantial increase among the more affluent segments of our economy.

Data on income can be misleading unless attention is paid to the definition of income and what is excluded. Households may be income-poor and asset-wealthy.

A study of spendable discretionary income (SDI) using 1981 data found that over 25 million households, about 31 percent, had DI, accounting for 51 percent of after-tax income. About 28 percent of after-tax income was SDI and by 1990 SDI is projected to be about $325 billion in 1980 dollars, an increase of almost two-thirds. Households with income of $50,000 and over are but 17 percent of the total but have over 46 percent of spendable disposable income.

Poverty exists amid affluence. About 15 percent of the population, 35.3 million people in 1983, were reported to be living in poverty. If the value of noncash benefits is included, then estimates are significantly lower, ranging from 10 to 13.7 percent of the population.

Income projections using census data and an average annual growth rate of 1.5 and 2.0 percent show a large increase in affluent and superaffluent households. The number of households with incomes below $25,000 will remain about the same in 1995 as it was in 1980, the $50,000-and-over category will increase 150 percent from 1980 to 1995, and the number of $25,000-and-under households will, for the first time, equal the number of $25,000-and-over households. Also, it should be noted that a large proportion of the latter are singles' households representing a higher proportion of SDI than would be the case for under $25,000 husband–wife households. They need not represent the underprivileged.

The future income picture in general is one of increasing and mass affluence. Most of the household growth is projected in the $35,000-and-over income brackets, particularly among middle-aged households, the 35–54-year-old households.

By 1995, the superaffluent households, those with incomes of $50,000 and over in 1980 dollars, will control a larger proportion of our discretionary income and afford very affluent living standards. Mass affluence will be particularly prevalent among husband–wife households, and as families decrease in size there will be per-capita income gains. The widespread affluence suggests the affordability of luxury life-styles by broader segments of society—more democratic affluence. Marketers would do well to keep the wants and desires of affluent and superaffluent middle-aged husband–wife households in focus.

When 1941 consumer expenditures are compared with those of 1980 a significantly smaller proportion was spent on food and beverages and about one-half as much on alcohol and clothing. However, proportionate expenditures on medical care more than doubled; transportation expenditures increased by almost 40 percent.

References

Bureau of the Census. 1979. *Population Estimates and Projections. Current Population Reports.* Series P-25, no. 805 (May).

———. 1984. *Money, Income, and Poverty Status of Families and Persons in the United States.* No. 145 (p. 60).

———. 1981. *Money Incomes of Families and Persons in the United States: 1979.* Series P-60, no. 129.

———. 1985. *Estimates of Poverty Including the Value of Noncash Benefits: 1984.* Technical Paper no. 52.

Bureau of Labor Statistics. 1983. *1980–81 Consumer Expenditure Survey.* Department of Labor, 83-235.

Forbes. 1983. "America's 30 Richest" (Fall):132.

Lazer, William. 1984. "How Rising Affluence Will Reshape Markets." *American Demographics* (February).

Linden, Fabian, Gordon W. Green, Jr., and John F. Coder. No date. *A Marketer's Guide to Discretionary Income.* Consumer Research Center and Bureau of the Census.

New York Times. 1986. "The Average Guy Takes It on the Chin" (13 July): Business, p. 1.

U.S. News and World Report. 1983. "America's Richest: 15 Billionaires" (10 October):95.

Wall Street Journal. 1983. "More Affluence" (24 March):29.

3
Employment Trends and Developments

Introduction

Information about emerging employment trends is used to develop strategic plans for business, labor, and public policy. But labor force projections and forecasts are often imprecise and uncertain. Some statements can be made with relative confidence, such as the proportionate increases among 25–54-year-old workers, the decline of the 16–24-year-old group, and the increase in future dependency ratios. Others are questionable, such as predictions about the number of barbers, bellhops, and brokers that will be required in 1995. Even so, the use of various models to arrive at specific projections by occupations can indeed prove useful for planning purposes (Bureau of Labor Statistics 1984, p. 2).

The future availability of jobs, especially appropriate jobs, concerns people worldwide. Jobs are determinants of individual and societal economic well-being because they govern income and demand. They power future markets for products and services. Business, labor, and government keep a careful eye on monthly unemployment statistics and general employment trends.

Rising unemployment rates since the mid-1960s have made people in the United States more sensitive to occupational developments. Since the 1960s, unemployment in the United States has generally moved in an upward direction, reaching new highs with each economic downturn. The unemployment rate in the United States rose from 5.6 percent in 1974 to 9.7 percent in 1982, generally fluctuating in a range from 7 to 7.7 percent—a high figure indeed. Despite high unemployment, the actual numbers in the labor force increased rapidly from 82 million in 1970 to 110 million in 1982 (Morrison 1983).

Jobs are now referred to as among the basic human rights, along with food, housing, clothing, education, and medical care. They are central to a society's well-being.

We shall briefly investigate trends in the labor-force pool and future job opportunities. The likely impact of changes in demographics, on working women, particularly wives, on high-tech industries, and on declining and growth industries will be discussed. Attention will be directed to the growth prospects for various occupations and industries, particularly the high-tech and service industries.

Readers should bear in mind an important caveat. Labor-force considerations are so broad and diverse that only a few areas of interest to marketers will be covered in a limited way. Those interested will find a host of government publications containing a wealth of data about most of the specialized employment areas they would like to investigate in depth.

Demographics and Labor-force Developments

The demographic trends discussed in chapter 1, such as the aging of our baby-boom population, with their shift from ages of labor-force entry into prime working ages, will make themselves felt in the next decade. By 1990 most of the baby boomers will be in the 35–44-year age group. Their employment aspirations and needs will place increasing pressure on upper management and executive-level jobs as mid-career goals are brought into focus. They will continue to demand entry into the executive suites and will be impatient with older executives who are blocking them. At the same time the number of new labor-force entrants will shrink in the 1980s, easing pressures on entry-level jobs. That was the very pressure that characterized the 1970s, when millions of unskilled younger workers were being absorbed.

The U.S. labor force in 1984 was estimated at 114 million, made up of 64 million men (56 percent) and 50 million women (44

Table 3–1
Labor-force Growth by Sex, Age, and Race

	Actual			*Projected*	
Group	*1975*	*1980*	*1984*	*1990*	*1995*
Total, 16 years and over (thousands)	93,775	106,940	113,544	122,653	129,168
Men	56,299	61,453	63,835	67,146	69,282
16–24	12,371	13,606	12,727	11,163	10,540
25–54	34,991	38,712	42,302	48,079	51,200
55+	8,938	9,135	8,805	7,904	7,542
Women	37,475	45,487	49,704	55,507	59,886
16–24	10,250	11,696	11,260	10,089	9,623
25–54	21,860	27,888	32,360	39,632	44,519
55+	5,365	5,904	6,084	5,786	5,744
White	82,831	93,600	98,492	105,467	110,086
Black	9,263	10,865	12,033	13,602	14,796
Total, 16 years and over (percent)	100.0	100.0	100.0	100.0	100.0
Men	60.0	57.5	56.2	54.7	53.6
16–24	13.2	12.7	11.2	9.1	8.2
25–54	37.3	36.2	37.3	39.2	39.2
55+	9.5	8.5	7.8	6.4	5.8
Women	40.0	42.5	43.8	45.3	46.4
16–24	10.9	10.9	9.9	8.2	5.8
25–54	23.3	26.1	28.5	32.3	34.5
55+	5.7	5.5	5.4	4.7	4.4
White	88.3	87.5	86.7	86.0	85.2
Black	9.9	10.2	10.6	11.1	11.5

Source: Fullerton 1985.

percent). It is projected to continue the slowdown in growth that began in the 1970s. Table 3–1 presents data on the growth of the labor force from 1970, with projections to 1995, broken down by sex, age, and race. The civilian labor force is projected to reach 129.2 million people by 1995, a growth of 20 percent from 1980. By then, men will account for only 53.6 percent of the total, versus 46.4 percent for women. The average labor-force growth rate is estimated at 1.3 percent per year till 1990, when it will slow to 1.0 percent until 1995 (Fullerton 1985, pp. 17–18).

The women's component will grow at a faster rate than the overall labor force—accounting for over two-thirds of the growth.

About 20 percent of the labor-force growth will be accounted for by blacks (Morrison 1983; Fullerton 1985). Although the faster growth of the black labor force, as compared with the white labor force, is projected to continue, they will still account for less than 12 percent of the 1995 total.

Aging Labor Force

Table 3–2 presents a more detailed breakdown of the labor force by age for 1982 and 2000. In 1982, persons aged 18–24 made up about 20 percent of the total labor force; those 25–34 were 28 percent; those 35–54 were 35 percent; while the 55 and over group were but 14 percent. About 3 million of those 55 and over, or 2.7 percent, were over 65, three-fourths of them in the 65 to 74 age group.

Note the dramatic changes projected for the year 2000, which mirror population changes in general. The proportion of younger persons in the labor force is projected to decline significantly, while the middle-aged workers, those 35–54, are projected to increase most dramatically, both proportionately and in number, growing from 39 million persons, or 35 percent, to 64 million persons, or 49 percent. One-half of the labor force will be in the middle-aged group and those in the prime working age group, 25–54, are projected to grow much faster than the total work force, increasing from 63 to 71 percent of the total.

Table 3–2
Labor Force by Age: 1982 and 2000

	% of Labor Force	
Age	*1982*	*2000*
18–24	20	15
25–34	28	22
35–54	35	49
55+	14	11

Source: Morrison 1983, p. 15.

These shifts should affect productivity favorably for two reasons. First, during the 1970s, the labor force absorbed a larger number of very young and unskilled workers. Second, the 25–54 group tend to be more mature, better educated, more experienced, and better trained than previous 25–54-year-old groups and than the 16–24-year-olds who made up a large share of the 1970s' labor-force growth.

The older members of the labor force, those 55 and over, will realize a 3-percent decline, and even with the greying and aging of the United States, only 2 percent of the labor force is expected to be 65 and over in 2000. Despite an increase in the number of older persons by the year 2000, there will continue to be a decline in the proportion attracted to the labor force as the trend to early retirement continues. For men the decline is expected to be both relative and absolute; women are expected to maintain a relatively constant labor force participation rate.

Dependency Ratio and Retirement

As is shown in table 3–3 the median age of the labor force, which declined from 1960 on, will rise again over the next 15 years. It fell in the 1960s and 1970s because of the large number of the baby boomers and women who entered the labor force. But from 1982 on the labor force will age with a continuation of a higher median age of male versus female workers and white versus black and other workers.

Table 3–3
Median Age of the Labor Force

	1950	*1960*	*1970*	*1982*	*1990*	*1995*
All Participants	38.6	40.5	39.0	34.8	35.9	37.3
Men	39.3	40.5	39.4	35.3	36.4	37.8
Women	36.7	40.4	38.3	34.2	35.3	36.8
White	—	40.7	39.3	35.0	36.1	37.5
Black and Other	—	38.2	36.6	32.8	34.8	36.3

Source: Fullerton and Tschetter 1983, p. 6.

Labor-force age has an effect on the dependency ratio, which refers to the number of persons not in the labor force per one hundred persons that are. The ratio declined sharply in the 1970s as baby boomers and women entered the work force. It is expected to decline further in the near future, but at a slower rate, reflecting the increasing ranks of working women. The ratio declined from 142.8 in 1955 to 104.5 in 1984, and is projected to decrease significantly to 98.4 in 1995.

However, when those who are not in the labor force (numerator) are grouped into three categories, those under 16, those 16 to 64, and those 65 and over, and the relationships between the last two groups are considered, an interesting picture emerges. The increasing burden of providing for the retirement and care of older workers comes into clearer focus.

The drop in the 16–64 age group dependency ratio reflects the entry of women into the labor force. Also, the ratio for those under 16 was higher in 1955 and 1965 reflecting baby boom births, but dropped when that generation entered the work force. However, the dependency ratio for older people has grown, and this reflects both the aging population and lower labor-force participation rates. Although the older group accounts for the smallest portion of the "dependents," their costs per person are estimated at three times that of other groups (Fullerton 1985, p. 23).

Management is challenged to consider implications of an aging and greying work force. Conjectures may be made that the projected decline in people aged 16–24 will increase the demand for older workers. On the other hand, such factors as high unemployment, automation, increasing productivity, international competition, women in the work force, and immigration may place added pressure on older workers to retire earlier. Will future economic conditions pressure them to continue working? Will additional laws be passed forcing compulsory retirement of older workers? Will there be a shortage of young unskilled workers for companies in such sectors as supermarkets and fast foods? Though the future outcomes may not be clear, it is obvious that the aging work force will have important economic and social implications for such important considerations as employee benefits, pension plans, work schedules, and company personnel policies.

Retirement is an important social issue as a result of the aging of the population and the decline in work activity of older men. These shifts are coupled with rising life expectancy, thus adding to the pressures that increase intergenerational conflicts, particularly during periods of high unemployment. As older workers block the advancement of younger and newer labor-force entrants, conflicts arise. On the other hand, since 1963, the labor-force participation rates for men 55 and over have declined continuously in every age category.

The statistics indicate that older workers generally want to retire and do so at an earlier age although a limited number continue to work full time. Despite a growing and aging work force overall, the number of older labor-force participants has remained quite stable since 1950. (Morrison 1983, p. 16). Although many workers might like to ease into retirement or work part time, the lack of flexible employment policies, the lack of suitable work, and age discrimination do not encourage it. A retirement choice becomes a permanent decision, and once it is made, relatively few retirees seem to return to the labor force.

Job Prospects: Consumer Expenditures

Predicting future job prospects is a trying task, replete with opportunities for error. We shall try and develop some perspectives of future employment opportunities by first considering projections of consumer expenditures on products and services that should indicate where industry opportunities lie, and then by detailing employment projections by industry. We shall also pay attention to the services sector and to occupations with the highest and lowest growth potential.

Table 3–4 presents projected consumer dollar expenditures, in 1972 dollars, by product and service categories. As consumer expenditures increase in a sector, one could reason, so will that sector's job opportunities, but this need not follow. Between 1982 and 1995, expenditures on durable goods will increase by $100 billion, on nondurables by $104 billion, and on services by a striking $238 billion. Consumer expenditures on services are expected to equal those on goods by 1995.

Table 3–4
Personal Consumption Expenditures by Major Categories Projected to 1995
(1972 $ billion)

Category	*1977*	*1982*	*1990*	*1995*
Total	$864.3	$970.2	$1,240.2	$1,412.0
Motor vehicles and parts	63.5	57.4	90.3	98.2
Household appliances	26.3	33.0	48.3	57.4
Household furnishings	26.6	26.7	37.5	45.1
Other durable goods	21.5	22.7	32.7	39.7
Total durables	138.0	139.8	208.8	240.4
Food and beverages	170.6	184.0	213.2	223.8
Clothing and shoes	67.5	84.4	103.9	113.7
Gasoline and oil	27.7	25.6	28.8	28.9
Fuel oil and coal	4.4	3.5	3.7	4.4
Other nondurable goods	63.2	66.6	86.6	97.2
Total nondurables	333.4	364.2	436.2	468.0
Housing services	141.3	171.3	212.7	247.7
Household electricity	16.0	18.3	24.6	28.4
Household natural gas	6.5	6.6	5.1	4.7
Other household operations	32.6	38.6	52.9	64.0
Transportation services	32.7	31.7	42.4	50.1
Other services	163.9	199.6	257.5	309.1
Total services	393.0	466.2	595.2	704.0

Source: Andreassen et al. 1983, p. 18.

The percentage distribution of personal consumption expenditures on durables will increase from 14.4 percent of total expenditures in 1982 to 17.0 percent in 1995. The proportion spent on nondurables, however, will fall from 37.5 to 33.1 percent. Services, as expected, will grow from 48.0 to 49.8 percent. The biggest proportionate change occurs in expenditures on food and beverages, which will drop from 19.0 to 15.8 percent by 1995.

Employment by Industry Sector and Occupation

Table 3–5 considers changes in employment by economic sector from 1959 to 1995. Agriculture, mining, nondurable goods manufacturing, and private households are projected to show decreases. The largest annual average rates of change in employment are in services, trade (wholesaling and retailing) and finance, insurance and real estate. From 1984 to 1995, service jobs are projected to grow by about 9 million, followed by trade with 5.3 million. Agriculture will show a loss of more than 200,000 jobs.

The U.S. economy is undergoing major restructuring that is influencing present and future job opportunities. As has been emphasized, the service-producing industries, particularly the services sector, have accounted for an ever-increasing proportion of the new jobs.

The goods-producing industries have declined in importance as employers. In the 25-year period from 1959 to 1984 the United States added almost 40 million jobs. Table 3–6 shows the changing occupational structure in the United States from 1973 to 1984, with projections to 1995. The largest projected percentage change in employment between 1984 and 1995 is among the three occupational groups having the largest proportion of college-educated workers or postsecondary trainees, namely, executive, administrative and managerial; professional; and technical. Along with sales and service workers, their growth rate will exceed the overall average. Technicians and related support workers have the highest projected rate, 28.7 percent, which is a slowing of the 58 percent growth rate from 1973 to 1984. They are followed by service workers with 21.3 percent.

Administrative support workers, including clerical, are expected to add 1.8 million jobs and remain the largest overall group. They will, however, continue to feel the effects of office automation.

Service workers are projected to account for 3.3 million of the 16 million job increase, 20 percent, more than any other group. This reflects a continuing shift in our economy from goods production to services production.

Farming, forestry, and fishing employment are expected to continue their decline. The rate of decline will slow, however, to about

Table 3–5
Employment by Major Sector: 1959–95
(in thousands)

	Employment									
	Actual				*Projected*					
					1990			*1995*		
Economic Sector	*1959*	*1969*	*1979*	*1984*	*Low*	*Moderate*	*High*	*Low*	*Moderate*	*High*
Total	67,784	81,508	101,471	106,841	112,797	116,865	119,020	117,268	122,760	127,719
Agriculture	5,583	3,622	3,340	3,293	3,125	3,164	3,201	2,971	3,059	3,128
Nonagriculture	62,201	77,886	98,131	103,548	109,672	113,701	115,819	114,297	119,700	124,591
Government (including enterprises)	8,083	12,195	15,947	15,984	16,465	16,596	16,795	16,820	17,144	17,592
Federal	2,233	2,758	2,773	2,807	2,790	2,790	2,790	2,800	2,800	2,800
State and local	5,850	9,437	13,174	13,177	13,675	13,806	14,005	14,020	14,344	14,792
Private	54,118	65,691	82,184	87,564	93,207	97,105	99,024	97,477	102,556	106,999
Mining	614	501	704	651	633	659	676	600	631	661
Construction	3,910	4,374	5,879	5,920	5,910	6,189	6,276	6,331	6,636	6,856
Manufacturing	17,018	20,467	21,401	19,779	20,063	20,913	21,320	20,089	21,124	22,037
Durable	9,582	12,080	12,985	11,744	12,349	12,872	13,122	12,568	13,216	13,788
Nondurable	7,436	8,387	8,416	8,035	7,714	8,041	8,198	7,521	7,908	8,249
Transportation, communications, and public utilities	4,255	4,637	5,414	5,500	5,726	5,957	6,065	5,996	6,304	6,586
Trade	13,492	16,671	22,311	24,290	25,991	27,106	27,706	26,848	28,272	29,545
Finance, insurance, and real estate	2,959	3,859	5,514	6,296	6,699	6,991	7,146	7,024	7,397	7,716
Services	9,591	13,326	19,635	23,886	27,080	28,142	28,662	29,607	31,170	32,537
Private households	2,279	1,856	1,326	1,242	1,106	1,148	1,174	982	1,023	1,060

Source: Personick 1985, p. 28.

Table 3–6
Employment by Occupation: 1984 and 1995

	1984		*1995*		*% Change in Employment*	
Occupation	*Number*	*Percent*	*Number*	*Percent*	*1973–84*	*1984–95*
Total employment	106,843	100.0	122,760	100.0	23.4	14.9
Executive administrative, and managerial workers	11,274	10.6	13,762	11.2	48.4	22.1
Professional workers	12,805	12.0	15,578	12.7	46.2	21.7
Technicians and related support workers	3,206	3.0	4,119	3.4	58.3	28.7
Salesworkers	11,173	10.5	13,393	10.9	41.5	19.9
Administrative support workers, including clerical	18,716	17.5	20,499	16.7	24.7	9.5
Private household workers	993	0.9	811	0.7	−27.0	−18.3
Service workers, except private household workers	15,589	14.6	18,917	15.4	37.6	21.3
Precision production, craft, and repair workers	12,176	11.4	13,601	11.1	20.2	11.7
Operators, fabricators, and laborers	17,357	16.2	18,634	15.2	−7.2	7.3
Farming, forestry, and fishing workers	3,554	3.3	3,447	2.8	−5.9	−3.0

Source: Silvestri & Lukasiewicz 1985, p. 43.

3 percent, one-half the rate between 1973 and 1984 (Silvestri & Lukasiewicz 1985, pp. 42–43).

The twenty occupations with the largest projected growth between 1982 and 1995 are shown in table 3–7. In terms of total number of jobs, building custodians, cashiers, and secretaries head the list, all adding over 700,000 jobs. The top ten fall into the least prestigious segments of the service sector.

When the rate of growth is considered, computer industry jobs exhibit the fastest growth. Computer service technicians head the

Table 3–7
Twenty Occupations with Largest Job Growth: 1982–95

Occupation	*Change in Total Employment (thousands)*	*% of Total Job Growth*	*% Change*
Building custodians	779	3.0	27.5
Cashiers	744	2.9	47.4
Secretaries	719	2.8	29.5
General clerks, office	696	2.7	29.6
Sales clerks	685	2.7	23.5
Nurses, registered	642	2.5	48.9
Waiters and waitresses	562	2.2	33.8
Teachers, kindergarten and elementary	511	2.0	37.4
Truck drivers	425	1.7	26.5
Nursing aides and orderlies	423	1.7	34.8
Sales reps, technical	386	1.5	29.3
Accountants, auditors	344	1.3	40.2
Automotive mechanics	324	1.3	38.3
Supervisors, blue-collar workers	319	1.2	26.6
Kitchen helpers	305	1.2	35.9
Guards and doorkeepers	300	1.2	47.3
Food preparation and service workers, fast food restaurants	297	1.2	36.7
Managers, store	292	1.1	30.1
Carpenters	247	1.0	28.6
Electrical and electronic technicians	222	0.9	60.7

Source: Rosenthal 1985, p. 8.

list with a projected growth rate of about 97 percent from 1982 to 1995. As table 3–8 shows, computer-related services account for 4 of the top 6 categories and the services sector is very heavily represented.

But, merely considering the fastest growing occupations can be quite misleading, for many categories are small numerically and do

Table 3–8
Twenty Fastest Growing Occupations: 1982–95

Occupation	*% Projected Employment Growth*
Computer service technicians	96.8
Legal assistants	94.3
Computer systems analysts	85.3
Computer programmers	76.9
Computer operators	75.8
Office machine repairers	71.7
Physical therapy assistants	67.8
Electrical engineers	65.3
Civil engineering technicians	63.9
Peripheral electronic data processing equipment operators	63.5
Insurance clerks, medical	62.2
Electrical and electronic technicians	60.7
Occupational therapists	59.8
Surveyor helpers	58.6
Credit clerks, banking and insurance	54.1
Physical therapists	53.6
Employment interviewers	52.5
Mechanical engineers	52.1
Mechanical engineering technicians	51.6
Compression and injection mold machine operators, plastics	50.3

Source: Rosenthal 1985, p. 9.

not change the overall distribution of workers by earning levels. A list of the ten fastest growing and most rapidly declining industries, along with industries projected to provide the most new jobs from 1984 to 1995, is given in table 3–9. Business services, retail trade, and eating and drinking places, the top three in new job creation, are projected to add about one-half of the new jobs. The two fastest growing industries in terms of annual rates of change in employment are in services, medical and business, followed by computers and peripheral equipment, and material handling equipment. One-half of the ten fastest growing industries are in the services sector.

Table 3–9
Projected Changes in Employment by Industry: 1984–95

Most New Jobs	*Employment Gain (thousands)*
Business services	2,633
Retail trade, except eating and drinking places	1,691
Eating and drinking places	1,203
Wholesale trade	1,088
Medical services, n.e.c.	1,065
Professional services, n.e.c.	1,040
New construction	558
Doctors' and dentists' services	540
Hotels and lodging places	385
Credit agencies and financial brokers	382
Fastest Growing	*% Average Annual Rate of Change*
Medical services, n.e.c.	4.3
Business services	4.2
Computers and peripheral equipment	3.7
Materials handling equipment	3.7
Transportation services	3.5
Professional services, n.e.c.	3.5
Scientific and controlling instruments	2.9
Medical instruments and supplies	2.8
Doctors' and dentists' services	2.6
Plastics products	2.5
Most Rapidly Declining	*% Average Annual Rate of Change*
Cotton	−4.2
Wooden containers	−3.6
Leather products including footwear	−2.8
Iron and ferroalloy ores mining	−2.7
Sugar	−2.7
Leather tanning and finishing	−2.6
Railroad transportation	−2.6
Nonferrous metal ores mining, except copper	−2.6
Dairy products	−2.3
Blast furnaces and basic steel products	−2.2

Source: Personick 1985, p. 31.

The most rapidly declining industries are cotton, wooden containers, leather products, and iron and ferroalloy ores mining.

Services, Employment, and Earnings

Data on future industry employment and occupations have clearly shown a shift from goods-producing to service-producing industries. In a sense, the United States has been a service economy for over 30 years (Urquhart 1984, p. 15). The Fisher–Clark hypothesis on economic development, which states that economic development results in a shift in employment from agriculture to goods-producing and then service-producing industries, seems to be supported by the data for the United States from 1850 to 1982, which are shown in table 3–10.

Agriculture made up a resounding 65 percent of all employment in 1850, but its share has dropped continuously to 3.6 percent in 1982. Services, on the other hand, which offered but 17.3 percent of total employment in 1850 have increased continuously to almost 70 percent. The goods sector has shown a relative decline since the 1950s, but in numbers, its employment has actually grown.

The service sector employs about 30 million persons, about 28 percent of all U.S. workers. That number is expected to grow to about 40 million, one-third of the U.S. labor force (Edwards & Snyder 1984, p. 4). The rapid growth of services and the decline of basic manufacturing industries has resulted in some interesting speculation about future employment and earnings. The basic manufacturing industries such as steel, automobiles, and heavy earthmoving equipment have been in a state of relative decline. They are among the most unionized industries with the highest pay rates. Their decline has been variously described as the deindustrialization of the United States, the decline of the smokestack industries, and the fall of the rust bowl. This signifies the disappearance of many well-paying manufacturing jobs and increasing unemployment coupled with the rise of lower-paying jobs in the services sector. As a result, speculation is raised about the disappearance or decline of the U.S. middle class, a driving force behind U.S. marketing success.

Will the middle class be as adversely affected by the shift to services as has often been forecast? It could be, as some suggest,

Table 3–10
Percentage Distribution of Employment by Major Sector: 1850–1982

Year	*Agriculture*	*Goods-producing*	*Service-producing*
1850	64.5	17.7	17.8
1860	59.9	20.1	20.0
1870	50.8	25.0	24.2
1880	50.6	25.1	24.3
1890	43.1	28.3	28.6
1900	38.0	30.5	31.4
1910	32.1	32.1	35.9
1920	27.6	34.6	37.7
1930	21.8	31.7	46.6
1940	18.3	33.1	48.6
1952	11.3	35.5	53.3
1957	9.8	34.3	56.0
1962	7.8	33.1	59.1
1967	5.3	34.7	60.1
1972	4.4	31.4	64.2
1977	3.7	29.7	66.6
1979	3.6	30.2	66.3
1982	3.6	27.2	69.2

Source: Urquhart 1984, p. 16.

that the negative consequences of increases in services has been overplayed. First, the growth of the middle class in the past has been associated with the strong growth of services. Second, there is great interdependence among the goods and services sectors, with growth in one being related to growth in the other (Urquhart 1984, p. 15). Third, once the heavy industries are cut back and realistically re-aligned to meet market opportunities, it could be that growth will once again ensue.

But it must be noted that the past growth of the middle class that associated with services occurred while there was also strong growth in goods production and while imports were less important. Foreign competition could result in the future overseas growth in heavy industries.

Publications presaging the decline of the middle class point out that more new jobs are being created at the top and bottom of the earning structure, resulting in a two-tiered society. And with fewer advancement opportunities for those lower on the earning ladder, political and social unrest will be heightened and the purchasing stimulus of the great U.S. middle class will decline.

But data on changes in occupational structure and wages of the past decade do not seem to support this thesis. In the future, professional and technical workers, as well as craft workers who have higher-than-average levels of earnings, are projected to grow and the largest occupational groups with lower-than-average incomes are projected to decline as a proportion of total employment. The proclaimed bipolarization does not seem likely by 1995. In other words, the middle class will likely hold its own (Rosenthal 1985, pp. 6–9).

Although a transition has indeed occurred, it is expected that employment in heavy manufacturing will actually increase over the next 15 years. Between 1982 and 1995, job gains in manufacturing will comprise 1 of 6 jobs. (Personick 1983, p. 34). And though manufacturing jobs fell from 25 to 19 percent of all jobs from 1959 to 1984, that share is expected to remain stable. Factory employment is projected to add 3 million jobs from 1982 to 1990, and another 1.3 million from 1990 to 1995. But it also seems that employment in several key industries, such as autos and steel, which is affected by productivity and technological advancement, will not regain previous job levels.

The service-producing industries are expected to continue to account for most of the new job growth from 1982 to 1995. They are often classified into transportation, communications, public utilities, trade, finance, insurance, real estate, government, and others categories. The "others" category is very interesting for it is expected to grow the fastest since it includes medical care, business, professional and personal services, hotels, and nonprofit organizations. This group will likely account for 1 of 3 new jobs created from 1982 to 1995 and will be less volatile for it is less affected by cyclical swings (Morrison 1983; Personick 1983).

Data indicate that the shift in employment to services reflects not so much a migration of workers from goods producing to services sectors. Rather, it reflects the expansion of the labor force into services, especially the participation of women (Urquhart 1984, p. 20).

High-tech Industries

Most states affected by the decline of the so-called smokestack industries, set out to attract high-tech industries to replace lost jobs. Although high-tech industries vary widely, they usually emphasize R&D expenditures, use scientific and technical personnel, and deal with sophisticated products. Employment data indicate that although high-tech employment is expected to grow somewhat faster than the economy as a whole, nevertheless high-tech industries overall will still account for but a small proportion of new jobs. Even when high-tech is defined very broadly, it will only account for approximately 17 percent of all new jobs between 1982 and 1995. In some states and communities, however, high-tech will continue to provide a significant proportion of new jobs. Six of 10 high-tech industries with the most job opportunities are located in the 10 most populous states (Richie, Hecker & Burgan 1983, p. 50).

Families and Employment

Families not only provide the country with the bulk of its labor supply, but shape the character of future workers. As families have changed from an extended to a nuclear system, and moved from rural to urban settings, labor market characteristics have also shifted.

Almost 85 percent of the labor force lived in families in 1982; while 9.6 percent lived alone, and 6.1 percent lived with nonrelatives. As table 3–11 shows, over one-third of the labor force (37 million) were husbands and one-fourth were wives (24.3 million). Moreover, there was a significant growth in multiearner families with more than 60 percent of husband–wife families having at least two persons employed, adding to their income and insulating them somewhat from economic downturns (Klein 1983).

About 52 percent of all wives and 79 percent of all husbands were in the labor force in 1983. The participation rate of husbands

Table 3–11
Labor Force, Unemployment, and Employment by Family Status: 1982 Annual Averages

Family Status	*Labor Force*	*Unemployment*	*Employment*
All persons	100.0%	100.0%	100.0%
In married-couple families:			
Husbands	36.0	23.3	37.4
Wives	23.2	17.1	23.8
Relatives	12.6	23.3	11.4
In families maintained by women:			
Women who maintain families	5.2	6.3	5.1
Relatives	4.4	11.4	3.7
In families maintained by men:			
Men who maintain families	1.7	1.7	1.7
Relatives	1.4	2.6	1.2
Persons living alone	9.5	7.0	9.7
All others	6.1	7.2	5.9

Source: Klein 1983, p. 22.

over time has declined steadily from 93 percent in 1940, reflecting a reduction in the number of working husbands 55 and over. This, in turn, stems from better private retirement plans, disability plans, and Social Security payments. The labor-force participation rate for husbands 65 and over fell sharply from 48 percent in 1952 to 19 percent (Waldman 1983, pp. 18–19).

Husbands and wives account for a lower proportion of the unemployed than they do of the labor force. Unemployment is a more difficult problem for families maintained by women who lack the cushioning effect of other employed members. And because blacks are more likely to live in families maintained by women than are whites or Hispanics, and are more likely to be the first laid off, they are more adversely affected by unemployment than the population at large.

A majority of all mothers with children under 6 were in the labor force in 1983, the first time this has happened (Waldman 1983). And this trend is expected to continue. A record number of mothers in 1984, 19.5 million, were in the labor force. Six out of

10 mothers with children under 18 were working mothers, just the reverse of 1974 when 6 out of 10 stayed at home. The majority of these mothers works full time and they do not tend to leave the labor force after childbirth. Nearly half the mothers with a child under 1 are in the work force (Hayghe 1984, p. 31).

The majority of children under 18, 56 percent of 58 million, had mothers in the labor force as compared with 39 percent in 1970. Most of the children were under 14, requiring some sort of day care. Half the children of two-parent families had both working mothers and fathers (Hayghe 1984, p. 32).

Thus, the majority of preschoolers will join the majority of school-age children in having working mothers. Increasingly, we shall have to address the issue of the demand for a variety of child-care services for both preschool and school children. The demand will continue to grow in the midst of the existing scarcity of quality care programs, particularly full-day programs. The greatest need is for child-care services for infants and toddlers because the labor-force participation rates for mothers of infants and toddlers is highest while the lack of services is most severe (Kamerman 1983).

Unions, Occupational Mobility, Education, and Self-Employment

There are many other topics about labor-force participants that we could investigate. We shall conclude with a brief note on unions, occupational mobility, education, and self-employment.

The proportion and number of workers covered by organized labor is not as large as most people assume, and has been declining steadily. Just between 1980 and 1984, organized labor lost an estimated 2.7 million members among employed wage and salary workers. This decline, moreover, took place during a period of strong work force growth.

The decline contrasts very sharply with the 1945–80 period, when union membership generally was rising (Adams 1985, p. 28). But the decline accentuates a trend to a decreasing proportion of union members among employed wage and salary workers that actually began in the late 1950s. The data reflect declines in employment in the heavily unionized goods-producing industries, the smokestack industries, such as steel and autos, as well as the effects

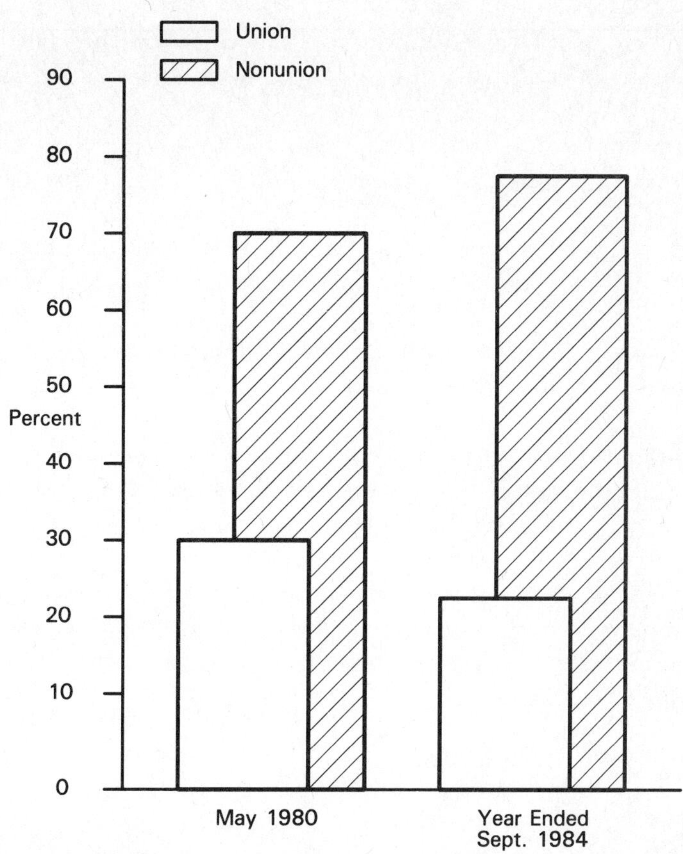

Source: Adams 1985, p. 28.

Figure 3–1. *Wage and salary workers, by union membership status: 1980–84*

of lost union jobs because of competition from exports and the recovery of industries with low levels of unionization.

In 1984, there were a reported 92.2 million wage and salary workers with 17.3 million belonging to unions. The total reporting either union members or coverage was 19.9 million (Bureau of Labor Statistics 1984, p. 13). As a percentage of the total wage and salary employment the unionization rate was 18.8 percent in terms of actual membership and 21.6 percent in terms of coverage. The union membership status of wage and salary workers for 1980 and 1984 is shown in figure 3–1.

A slightly different estimate established union membership in 1980 at 23.0 percent, dropping to 19.1 percent of all wage and salary employment in 1984 (Adams 1985, p. 25). Regardless, it is clear that union membership is less than one-fifth of the total and is falling. But there are large variations among occupations and industries.

U.S. workers in general are upwardly mobile. Occupational mobility is an important characteristic of U.S. life-styles, with the result that U.S. employees, as contrasted with those of other countries, such as Japan, are seen as job changers. But regardless of job switching, there is, nevertheless, considerable job stability among a large proportion of U.S. workers.

Data indicate that a large proportion of workers job shop initially and gain experience. Then, as middle-aged workers, they decide to spend the rest of their work life with one employer essentially pursuing the same type of job. Mature U.S. workers exhibit considerable job stability, for about one-third of all workers 45 and over have been with the same employer for 20 years or more. Another one-sixth have been with their employer for at least 15 years (Sehgal 1984, p. 18).

Education

As the baby boomers, those born between 1945 and 1964, complete their education and move into the labor force, the labor pool will have millions of additional workers with college degrees. The number of people receiving university degrees will continue to exceed a million per year for the rest of the 1980s. College graduates, as a result, will make up a larger proportion of the work force. In 1970, 1 in 7 workers completed college; in 1983, the ratio grew to 1 in 4. College graduates have higher labor-force participation rates than other groups, and bring added pressures for the more interesting and challenging jobs that permit them to realize themselves and utilize their capabilities (Young & Hayghe 1984).

Self-Employment

The proportion of the work force that is self-employed has been in a persistent and steady decline since 1980, falling from an amazing

60 percent to but 7 percent in 1970. This trend was supported by the shrinkage of the agricultural sector and fast growth of the industrial sector. For over a decade now, however, self-employment has been increasing and the prospects are that it will continue to do so for the remainder of this century.

The self-employed now account for 8.5 percent of the work force and are projected to grow to 10 percent by 1990 and 15 percent by 1995 (Edwards & Snyder 1984, p. 5). Entrepreneurship has been receiving greater attention and it is heightened by the growth of the services and information sectors. Increasing layoffs of executives, middle managers, and administrators results in a pool of experienced, capable people who are willing and able to start their own ventures. Many have experienced lucrative ventures in such high-tech industries as computer technology, bioengineering, and information systems. They are said to be the source of innovation and creativity, with companies such as Apple Computer setting an example.

References

Adams, Larry T. 1985. "Changing Employment Patterns of Organized Workers." *Monthly Labor Review* 108, no. 2 (February):25–31.

Andreassen, A. J., et al. 1983. "Economic Outlook for the 1990s: Three Scenarios for Growth." *Monthly Labor Review* 106, no. 11 (November):11–23.

Bureau of Labor Statistics. 1984. "Occupational Employment Projections through 1995." *Employment Projections through 1995*. Bulletin 21917.

Edwards, Gregg, and Dave Snyder. 1984. "Three Alternative Scenarios for Human Resource Development in America, 1980 to 2000." Unpublished paper.

Fullerton, Howard N., Jr. 1985. "The 1995 Labor Force: BLS' Latest Projections." *Monthly Labor Review* 108, no. 11 (November):17–25.

———, and John Tschetter. 1983. "The 1995 Labor Force: A Second Look." *Monthly Labor Review* 106, no. 11 (November):3–10.

Hayghe, Howard. 1984. "Working Mothers Reach Record Number in 1984." *Monthly Labor Review* 107, no. 12 (December):31–34.

Klein, Deborah Pistezner. 1983. "Trends in Employment and Unemployment in Families." *Monthly Labor Review* 106, no. 12 (December):21–25.

Kamerman, Sheila B. 1983. "Child Care Services: A National Picture." *Monthly Labor Review* 106, no. 12 (December):35–39.

Morrison, Malcolm H. 1983. "The Aging of the U.S. Population: Human Resource Implications." *Monthly Labor Review* 106, no. 5(May):13–19.

Moy, Joyanna. 1984. "Recent Labor Market Developments in the U.S. and Nine Other Countries." *Monthly Labor Review* 107, no. 1 (January):44–51.

Personick, Valerie A. 1983. "The Job Outlook through 1995: Industry Output and Employment." *Monthly Labor Review* 106, no. 11 (November):24–35.

———. 1985. "A Second Look at Industry Output and Employment." *Monthly Labor Review* 108, no. 11 (November):26–41.

Richie, Richard W., Daniel E. Hecker, and John W. Burgan. 1983. "High Technology Today and Tomorrow: A Small Slice of the Employment Pie." *Monthly Labor Review* 106, no. 11 (November):50–51.

Rones, Philip L. 1985. "Using the CPS to Track Retirement Trends among Older Men." *Monthly Labor Review* 108, no. 2 (February):46–49.

Rosenthal, Neil H. 1985. "The Shrinking Middle Class: Myth or Reality?" *Monthly Labor Review* 108, no. 3 (March):6–9.

Sehgal, Ellen. 1984. "Occupational Mobility and Job Tenure in 1983." *Monthly Labor Review* 107, no. 10 (October):18–22.

Silvestri, G. T., and J. M. Lukasiewicz. 1985. "Occupational Employment Projections: The 1984–95 Outlook." *Monthly Labor Review* 108, no. 11 (November):42–59.

Silvestri, George T., et al. 1983. "Occupational Employment Projections through 1995." *Monthly Labor Review* 106, no. 11 (November):37–49.

Urquhart, Michael. 1984. "The Employment Shift to Services: Where Did It Come From?" *Monthly Labor Review* 107, no. 4 (April):15–22.

Waldman, Elizabeth. 1983. "Labor Force Statistics from a Family Perspective." *Monthly Labor Review* 106, no. 12 (December):16–19.

Young, Ann McDougall, and Howard Hayghe. 1984. "More U.S. Workers Are College Graduates." *Monthly Labor Review* 107, no. 3 (March):46–49.

4
Geographic Shifts and Spatial Developments

Introduction

Retailers have long advocated that three factors should be considered carefully in establishing a business: location, location, and location. Where consumers live is of great importance in framing business strategies and decisions. The head of a well-established East Coast firm recalled in an executive seminar: "We woke up one morning to find that a major portion of our market is on the West Coast—thousands of miles and three time zones away!" Another remarked that regardless of popular conceptions, "a bulk of his market opportunities lies not in the major cities of the past but in the smaller areas of the West and South—they are the future."

In this chapter we shall briefly investigate information pertinent to such questions as: What have the population movements been in the United States? What regions of the country are projected to grow the fastest? Which areas will likely gain and which will likely lose population in the future? How will the largest cities likely fare? What are the projected fastest and slowest growing cities? Future business decisions and strategies should be framed bearing such geographic dynamics firmly in mind.

Geographic Center

The geographic center of our population has shifted steadily from the time of the first census taken in 1790 to the West and South, as

Source: Bureau of the Census 1985b, p. 8.

Figure 4–1. *Center of Population*

shown in figure 4–1. In 1790 it was located in Maryland and since then has pushed steadily through the Virginias, Ohio, Indiana, and Illinois. Currently, it is in the eastern sector of Missouri, having crossed the Mississippi River.

Overall population trends are clear and well established, as the thrust has been steady and persistent. Recent regional migration patterns have been quite predictable. The overall geographic trends of the 1960s, 1970s, and 1980s have mirrored each other as the South and West benefited while the Northeast and Northcentral areas did not. Intraregional migration developments, by contrast, have been quite unpredictable.

The Farm Scene

Although farmers are now having a difficult time, the productivity of the U.S. farmer has been a key ingredient in the economic success

Table 4–1
Farms and Farmland

Size of Farm (acres)	Number of Farms (thousands)					% Distribution: 1982	
	1959	1969	1974	1978	1982	Number of Farms	All Land in Farms
Total	3,711	2,730	2,314	2,258	2,241	100.0	100.0
Under 10	244	162	128	151	188	8.4	0.1
10–49	813	473	380	392	449	20.0	1.2
50–99	658	460	385	356	344	15.4	2.5
100–179	773	542	443	403	368	16.4	5.1
180–259	414	307	253	234	211	9.4	4.6
260–499	472	419	363	348	315	14.1	11.5
500–999	200	216	207	213	204	9.1	14.2
1000–1999	79	91	93	98	97	4.3	13.4
2000 +	57	60	62	63	65	2.9	47.4

Source: Bureau of the Census 1985b.

of the United States. At the turn of the century we were largely an agrarian society. The rural United States has undergone a major transition. In 1980, the farm population represented but 9 percent of the rural population. Our society has been transformed into an urban society, agriculture became one of our most productive technologies, and relatively few farms and farmers are able to feed not only the 240 million in the United States but untold millions abroad.

In 1930, the farm population was one-fourth of the total population. By 1985, it declined to 2.2 percent (Bureau of the Census 1985b, p. 633). Total farm population fell sharply from 30,529,000 to 5,355,000 people, who live on fewer farms and support growing populations. Much of the former farmland has been transformed into suburban residential areas, towns, cities, and shopping centers.

Between 1950 and 1985 (preliminary estimates), the number of farms shrunk by more than half—from 5,648,000 to 2,285,000. The acreage also decreased from 1,202,000 acres in 1950 to an estimated 1,016,000 acres, a decrease of over 15 percent. This means that the farm size more than doubled from 213 acres in 1950 to an estimated 445 acres in 1985 (Bureau of the Census 1985b, p. 635).

Table 4–2
Farms and Farm Acreage by Region: 1982

	Number of Farms		*All Land in Farms*	
Region	*Thousands*	*%*	*Millions of Acres*	*%*
Northeast	131	5.85	23.0	2.33
Midwest	932	41.59	354.2	35.89
South	896	39.98	293.8	29.77
West	280	12.49	315.7	31.99
Total	2,241		986.8	

Source: Bureau of the Census 1985b.

The trends also indicate that the largest farms, those of 2,000 acres or more, and those of between 1,000 and 1,999 acres, have shown continuous growth in numbers from 1959 to 1982. And while the former only accounted for 2.9 percent of all farms in 1982, they had 47.4 percent of all land in farms. Sixteen percent of the farms over 500 acres had 75 percent of all the farmland. Conversely, the number of small farms, those under 100 acres, and those under 500 acres, declined significantly and accounted for a relatively small proportion of all land in farms, as is shown in table 4–1. Sixty percent of the farms are less than 180 acres and they account for about 9 percent of all farmland (Bureau of the Census 1985b, p. 636).

Regionally, in 1982 the Midwest had both the largest number of farms and the largest farm acreage. The South had the second largest number of farms, followed by the West and Northeast. But, in terms of acreage, the West was second, followed by the South and Northeast. This is shown in table 4–2 (Bureau of the Census 1985, p. 637).

Where Do We Live?

Figure 4–2 traces the annual rate of population growth by region. The legend indicates the rate for each decade and the overall rate for the United States. The heavily shaded area indicates where the U.S. population is concentrated.

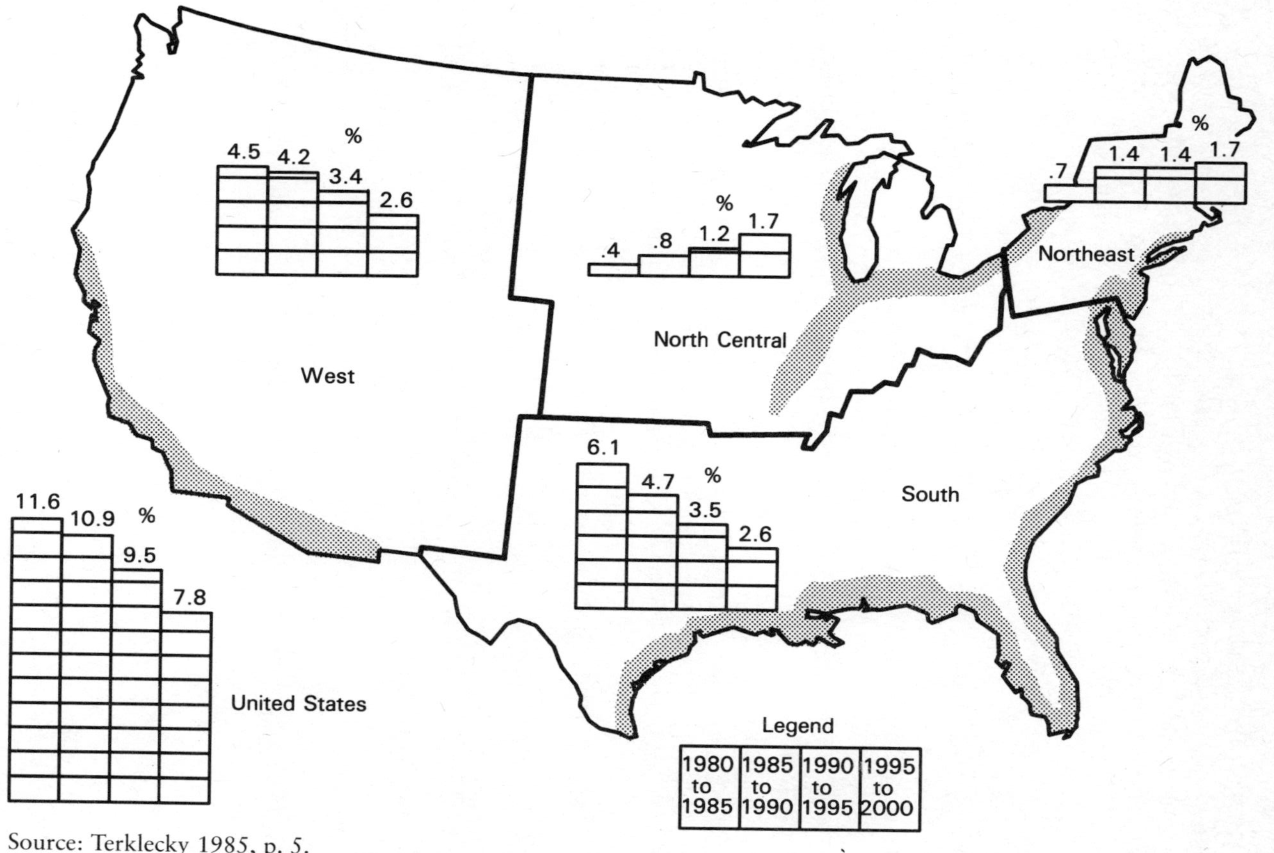

Source: Terklecky 1985, p. 5.

Figure 4–2. *Growth in Population, by Region: 1980–2000*

We live on a rather small proportion of the land mass of the United States, perhaps 5 percent, as the shaded area suggests. One can almost follow the water and develop a clear picture of population concentrations. Our population tends to congregate on a strip all down the eastern seaboard, from Boston through the east coast of Florida, up the west side of Florida and through the Gulf states to Texas. In the north, people cluster along the eastern extremities of the Great Lakes through Cleveland, Detroit, and Chicago, up to the west side of Lake Michigan and in a crescent from Chicago to St. Louis. On the West Coast the concentration starts above San Francisco and goes down to the Mexican border. Vast unpopulated areas of the United States exist, as people from crowded countries around the world, such as Japan, often note. The United States is, indeed, a large land mass compared with many European and Asian countries, spread out over thousands of miles, which results in costly and time-consuming distribution activities.

Although the United States has a lot of land, people seem to prefer the coasts and waterways to the plains; the West and South to the North; and the urban centers rather than totally rural areas; the Mountain and Southern states to the Northcentral plains. Though most of the U.S. population does not choose to live in the sparsely populated, colder areas of the northern tier, the inhabitants of these areas do not seem to mind and may actually be pleased with such general preferences. That permits them to enjoy the great outdoors, the wilderness, and the lack of crowding. And attempts to attract people to isolated, unpopulated areas, and to develop the employment opportunities necessary to support them, appear to have failed. The United States is an urban culture and although people profess to hating the problems of city living, they have not returned to the farm life. But they have moved to the suburbs, and to smaller towns and rural areas contiguous to large cities, heralding the shift to "ruralia."

State Population Trends

The top five states in percentage growth from 1970 to 1980 were Nevada, Arizona, Florida, Wyoming, and Utah, as is indicated in table 4–3. Nevada and Arizona had very high growth rates of 63.7

Table 4–3
Population Growth: 1970–80

State	*1980*	*1970*	*% Change*
Nevada	800,000	489,000	63.8
Arizona	2,718,000	1,755,000	53.1
Florida	9,746,000	6,791,000	43.5
Wyoming	470,000	332,000	41.3
Utah	1,461,000	1,059,000	37.9
Alaska	402,000	303,000	32.8
Idaho	944,000	713,000	32.4
Texas	14,229,000	11,199,000	27.1
California	23,668,000	19,900,000	18.5
Total U.S. population, 1970:	226,546,000		
Total U.S. population, 1980:	203,302,000		
Estimated U.S. population, 1990:	250,000,000[a]		
Estimated U.S. population, 2000:	268,000,000[a]		

Source: Bureau of the Census 1985b.
[a]Author's estimates.

and 53.1 percent respectively. Except for Florida, the fastest growth rates occur in states with relatively small population bases, such as Nevada. Between 1980 and 2000, Nevada may well continue to have the fastest growth rate of all states and projections are that its population will grow 59 percent between 1980 and 1990 and 50 percent from 1990 to 2000. But we must remember that in 1980 Nevada's total population was less than 800,000, not even that of our largest cities.

The changes in population by states between the 1970 and 1980 censuses are shown in table 4–3. The overall population, as was noted previously, grew 23 million from 203.3 million to 226.5 million. Although the largest percentage growth occurred in Nevada and Arizona, three states—Florida, California, and Texas—made up almost 10 million of the total 23 million increase. That is 41.7 percent of the total and underscores a migration from the snowbelt to the sunbelt, from the workbelt to the funbelt.

Projections indicate that these same three states are likely to account for the largest part of the growth through the year 2000.

Table 4–4
Leading States: Ranking by Population

State	*1980*	*2000*
California	1	1
Texas	3	2
Florida	7	3
New York	2	4

Source: Bureau of the Census 1985a.

Economic difficulties in Texas because of such occurrences as the unexpected severe drop in oil prices in the mid-1980s could well alter these results. Census projections of populations by states by the year 2000 indicate that California, Texas, and Florida are likely to account for over 50 percent of the growth. The projected rankings of these states is shown in table 4–4.

California will maintain its 1980 ranking as the most populous state of all. Texas will advance from third to second, while Florida will jump strikingly from seventh to third place. By contrast, New York state will fall behind and will drop from second to fourth, reflecting population migration out of the state.

The projected state population increases from 1980 to 2000 are Florida, 7.7 million; California, 6.9 million; and Texas, 6.5 million, for a total of 21.1 million. That represents almost 52 percent of the anticipated 41 million growth. Florida, California, and Texas are truly touchstone states that will permeate business decisions.

Regional Thrust

The Western and Southern population push has been noted. The West will continue to be the fastest growing U.S. region with a projected increase of 19 million people between 1980 and 2000, representing over 47 percent of the total population growth. By the year 2000 the West, with a projected growth rate of 22 percent between 1980 and 1990, and 18 percent between 1990 and 2000, will account for 23 percent of the total U.S. population.

The South will realize the second fastest regional growth. It will have well over one-third of the total U.S. population, 37 percent, by 2000. What important regional markets the South and West will represent!

The projected rate of increase of the South is slower than that of the West; 16 percent from 1980 to 2000, and 13 percent from 1990 to 2000. Its actual population increase, however, is an amazing 23 million, 57 percent of the total U.S. population growth for the period. The South will have risen again!

Several states and the District of Columbia are projected to show population losses from 1980 to 1990; these include Massachusetts, New York, Pennsylvania, and Ohio. The Northeastern region will be hard hit. From 1990 to 2000, Rhode Island, Connecticut, New Jersey, Illinois, Michigan, Iowa, and South Dakota are projected to join the population losers. The Northcentral and Northeastern states are over represented in this group. By the year 2000 the Northeast and South will have the oldest age distribution and the highest median ages in the United States, with the newer areas of the West, as might be expected, having the youngest.

Growth of Cities

There has been great turbulence in the growth of cities. Although the largest U.S. city is still New York with a 1982 population of 7,086,096, nevertheless, both the population and rankings of many of the 10 largest U.S. cities have changed substantially. Table 4–5 ranks the largest U.S. cities for 1970 and 1980 and indicates the percentage change for each. Though the ranking of the top four U.S. cities, New York, Chicago, Los Angeles, and Philadelphia remained the same between 1970 and 1980, it is significant that all except Los Angeles realized a decrease of more than 10 percent.

Between 1980 and 1984, however, the Northern cities such as Chicago and Philadelphia continued to lose population (New York gained 14,000 people), while the sunshine cities gained significantly. Los Angeles replaced Chicago as the second largest city, Houston took fourth place from Philadelphia, and San Antonio took tenth place from Baltimore, which dropped to twelfth. In just four years the cities of the South and West managed to increase in size substantially while the well-established large cities of the North and

Table 4–5
Largest Cities in the United States

	Rank 1970	*Rank 1980*	*% Change 1970–80*	*Rank 1984*
New York City	1	1	−10.4	1
Chicago	2	2	−10.8	3
Los Angeles	3	3	5.5	2
Philadelphia	4	4	−13.4	5
Houston	6	5	29.3	4
Detroit	5	6	−20.5	6
Dallas	8	7	7.1	7
San Diego	14	8	25.5	8
Phoenix	20	9	35.2	9
Baltimore	7	10	−13.1	12
San Antonio	15	11	20.1	10

Source: Bureau of the Census 1985a, p. 9.

Northeast declined. The clear patterns of the 1960s and 1970s have persisted (Bureau of the Census 1984a).

Figure 4–3 displays the location of metropolitan areas losing population between 1980 and 1984. The high concentration of them in the Midwest and Northeast stands out.

Suburban Developments

The largest cities, particularly the older ones, are often replete with the usual urban problems (including crime, decay, congestion, crowding, smog, and pollution) that stimulate population migration to the suburban and rural areas. Yet, some welcome gentrification has taken place and several cities are healing some of their ills. Urban residences appeal to certain population sectors such as the elderly who may have lived in an urban locale for a long time, and the single or childless young adults who enjoy the pace, pulse, entertainment, and cultural attractions of a large city. But it would be erroneous to conclude, as has been done, that people are moving back to the cores of cities, for they are not.

Source: Bureau of the Census 1984b.

Figure 4–3. *Location of Metropolitan Statistical Areas Losing Population: 1980–84*

Table 4–6
Crowded U.S. Cities: 1980

	Population	*Population per Square Mile*
New York City	7,071,639	23,455
Jersey City, N.J.	223,532	16,934
Paterson, N.J.	137,970	16,623
San Francisco	678,974	14,633
Newark, N.J.	329,248	13,662
Chicago	3,005,072	13,174
Philadelphia	1,688,210	12,413
Boston	562,994	11,928
Yonkers, N.Y.	195,351	10,675
Washington, D.C.	638,333	10,180
Miami	346,865	10,113

Source: Bureau of the Census 1985a, 1985b.

The urban areas need not represent preferred living spaces of most. The most crowded cities in terms of population per square mile lie in the Northeast, particularly New York and New Jersey. Only two crowded cities, Miami and San Francisco, are in the sunbelt, as shown in table 4–6, which lists the 10 most crowded U.S. cities of over 100,000 population in descending order of congestion.

In the development of large cities, the "doughnut" theory seems to apply—the hole in the center and growth around the outside. The major growth is not in the largest industrial cities, but rather in smaller towns and suburbs surrounding them. The cores of the cities are no longer the primary living and shopping areas they once were. The dominant positions they once occupied have changed. Some progress has been made in making downtown areas more attractive, but large cities continue to decline in population. Our largest cities do not even exhibit average U.S. population growth rates. The relentless push to the suburbs continues and as it does, the oldest suburbs will likely realize some of the ills that once affected only the city cores.

Urban growth may take place in concentric circles moving out

Table 4–7
Fastest Growing Cities of 100,000+: 1970–80

	1980 Population	*% Growth over 1970*
Anchorage, Alaska	174,431	262.8
Mesa, Ariz.	152,453	141.8
Aurora, Colo.	158,588	111.5
Lexington–Fayette, Ky.	204,165	88.8
Sterling Heights, Mich.	108,999	77.6
Arlington, Tex.	160,113	77.5
Modesto, Calif.	106,963	73.3
Garland, Tex.	138,857	70.5
Tempe, Ariz.	106,919	68.2
Colorado Springs, Colo.	215,150	58.8

Source: Bureau of the Census 1984b.

further and further from the city cores to the exurbs. Each of the communities in these rings will tend to be more self-contained with its own shopping, parks, recreation, and total life-style-supporting facilities and services. The need to return to the cores of cities for work or play has been permanently diminished. The cores of cities are more likely to be transient areas. Most go there to work in the morning and return to their suburban residences at night. In addition to residents, cities cater to "temporary residents," people visiting the city for conferences, conventions, and meetings, who then return to their home bases. To attract them, in some instances, cities offer casinos and gambling facilities. But city cores are no longer the hub for the living activities of the bulk of people. The cities are a haven for those who have not been able to escape and the transients, as well as the very well-to-do.

The smaller U.S. cities are considered to be more manageable and livable without many of the problems of larger metropolitan areas. Table 4–7 presents the 10 fastest growing cities with populations of 100,000 and over. Cities of less than 500,000 in population seem to best fit the living desires of most. In general, much of the rapid growth is in cities of less than 150,000 which are located in the sunbelt, contiguous to larger metropolitan areas. They reflect the desirable traits of space, clean air, quiet park-like surroundings, neighborliness, and livable climates. They represent ruralia—rural living with urban amenities.

By 2000 it is possible that 7 of the 10 largest U.S. cities will be in the sunbelt as people continue to "follow the water" and occupy but a very small proportion of the U.S. land mass. Effective marketing strategies and decisions will have to accommodate the geographic ebb and flow that is changing the face of the U.S. market.

Some growth cities such as Los Angeles, Miami, Dallas, and San Francisco are realizing an increasing international flavor. The Hispanic community in Los Angeles and the Cuban and Latin America flavor in Miami are examples. Various areas of cities are being influenced by Korean, Vietnamese, Japanese, and Philippine cultures. New immigrants are providing a source of semiskilled and skilled labor, entrepreneurship, creativity, a new vitality, and demand for housing. In particular, the West Coast and Pacific Rim locales are being affected and are benefiting from these new immigrants. These immigration thrusts are permanently changing the face of the U.S. market.

Metropolitan Areas

Although city rankings are used to measure population concentrations, two concepts that yield different results are metropolitan statistical areas (MSAs) and consolidated metropolitan statistical areas (CMSAs). The nation's top ten MSAs are shown in table 4–8, with population data from 1980 and 1984 (Bureau of the Census 1984b). New York with 17.8 million is by far the largest metropolitan area and Los Angeles, with 12.4 million, continues to rank second. Thirty-six metropolitan areas have populations of at least 1 million, and they comprise almost half our population covering only 5 percent of our land area. All of the fastest growing metropolitan areas from 1980 to 1984 were in the South and West, with the greatest total growth occurring in Los Angeles and Houston.

Metropolitan rankings can differ significantly from city rankings because some cities annex most of their suburbs while others maintain their corporate boundaries. San Antonio, for example, has annexed; Boston has not. The metropolitan areas in the past few

Table 4–8
The Largest Metropolitan Areas: 1984

	July 1, 1984		*April 1, 1980*		
Metropolitan Area	*Population (thousands)*	*Rank*	*Population (thousands)*	*Rank*	*% Change in Population 1980–1984*
New York–Northern New Jersey–Long Island, N.Y.–N.J.–Conn. CMSA	17,807	1	17,539	1	1.5
Los Angeles–Anaheim–Riverside, Calif. CMSA	12,373	2	11,498	2	7.6
Chicago–Gary–Lake County, Ill.–Ind.–Wis. CMSA	8,035	3	7,937	3	1.2
Philadelphia–Wilmington–Trenton, Pa.–N.J.–Del.–Md. CMSA	5,755	4	5,681	4	1.3
San Francisco–Oakland–San Jose, Calif. CMSA	5,685	5	5,368	5	5.9
Detroit–Ann Arbor, Mich. CMSA	4,577	6	4,753	6	−3.7
Boston–Lawrence–Salem, Mass.–N.H. CMSA	4,027	7	3,972	7	1.4
Houston–Galveston–Brazoria, Tex. CMSA	3,566	8	3,101	9	15.0
Washington, D.C.–Md.–Va. MSA	3,429	9	3,251	8	5.5
Dallas–Forth Worth, Tex. CMSA	3,348	10	2,931	10	14.2

Source: Bureau of the Census 1984b.

Note: CMSA = Consolidated Metropolitan Statistical Area; MSA = Metropolitan Statistical Area.

years seem to have grown at about the same rate as the country in general, reversing the slower rate of the 1970s. But whether this is indicative of a trend is not clear.

Summary

The geographic structure of markets has changed greatly over the past three decades. The geographic center of our population has shifted steadily from the time of the first census in 1790 to the South and West and is now located in eastern Missouri. The comment made famous by Greeley, "Go west, young man" seems to be most appropriate. As the United States has changed from a rural to an urban society, the productivity of U.S. farmers has increased. The rural United States, which is now encountering serious economic difficulties, has undergone a major transition. The total farm population fell from 25 percent of total population in 1930 to 2.2 percent in 1985. Since 1950 the number of farms has shrunk by more than one-half, as more of the farmland is given over to business, residential, and shopping center uses. The number of large farms has grown continuously and the small farms have shrunk so that farm size has more than doubled since 1950. Sixty percent of the farms now account for 9 percent of all farmland.

We live on less than 5 percent of the land mass of the United States, concentrated in a thin strip around the coasts and waterways. We prefer the urban to rural areas, the smaller towns contiguous to large cities, the mountain and southern states to the plains and Northeast. The top states in proportionate growth are the least populated states, such as Nevada, Arizona, Wyoming, and Utah. However, three states (Florida, California, and Texas) made up over 40 percent of the 1970s growth and are projected to account for over 50 percent of the 1980s growth. California will remain the most populous state; Florida will have the greatest increase in population.

The West and Southern population push will continue, with the West being the fastest growing area with a projected increase of 19 million people, 47 percent of the total projected growth. States such as Massachusetts, New York, Pennsylvania, and Ohio are projected to show losses between 1980 and 1990. By the year 2000 the

Northeast and South will have the oldest age distributions and highest median ages.

Although New York, Chicago, Los Angeles, and Philadelphia remain at the top of the list of large cities, the Northern cities in the top 10 are generally realizing declining populations, while the sunshine cities are growing. The urban areas do not represent the preferred living spaces, as crowding sends people to smaller areas contiguous to large cities. The smaller U.S. cities of under 500,000 seem to be most livable. By 2000, 7 of the 10 largest cities could well be in the sunbelt.

Some of our cities, such as Los Angeles, San Antonio, and San Francisco, are taking on the international flavor through other cultures, such as from Hispanics and Asians, reflecting immigration thrusts. The rapidly changing face of our geography reflects the need to reconsider location factors in marketing decisions.

References

Bureau of the Census. 1982. *Census of Agriculture.* Vol. 1.

———. 1984a. *CB:1984–85* (April):30.

———. 1984b. *The Nation's Largest Metropolitan Areas, 1982* (May):3.

———. 1984c. *Projections of the Population of the United States by Age, Sex, and Race: 1983–2080.* Series P-25, no. 952.

———. 1984d. *Statistical Abstract of the United States: 1985.* 105th ed.

———. 1985a. *Patterns of Metropolitan Areas and County Population Growth: 1980 to 1984.* Series P-25, no. 976.

———. 1985b. *Statistical Abstract of the United States: 1986.* 106th ed.

Terkleckyj, Nestor E. 1985. *Regional Growth in the United States.* NPA Data Services, Inc., Report no. 85-R-1.

Part II

Socioeconomic Dynamics

5
The American Mosaic: Minorities in Perspective

Diversity in the United States

The United States is hardly one nation. It has been described as nations within a nation; a polyglot of ethnic groups and races; a melting pot; and a mosaic of people from around the world. Garreau divided the United States into eight different nations, each with its unique, distinctive characteristics and focus, as is shown in figure 5–1: the Breadbasket, Empty Quarter, the Foundry, the Islands, Ectopia, Dixie, New England, and Mexamerica (Garreau 1981).

Marketers are very much interested in such diversity. They seek to segment markets and so identify profitable niches. Markets are segmented on the basis of a host of demographic, psychographic, sociographic, and economic factors. (Minorities made up the majority of the population in 25 U.S. cities of 100,000 or more in 1980 compared with only 9 cities in 1970. The top 10 cities where minorities are about two-thirds of the population in 1980 are shown in table 5–1.) In this chapter we explore some of the recent data relative to the racial and ethnic makeup of U.S. markets and focus on two important market segments: blacks and Hispanics (persons of Spanish origin may be of any race). Both groups are of sufficient number and different enough from the population at large in meaningful ways to warrant special attention by businesses. We shall discuss some of the important demographic features of each.

Any demographic portrait of the ancestral and racial makeup of the U.S. would highlight its diversity. Table 5–2 and figure 5–2

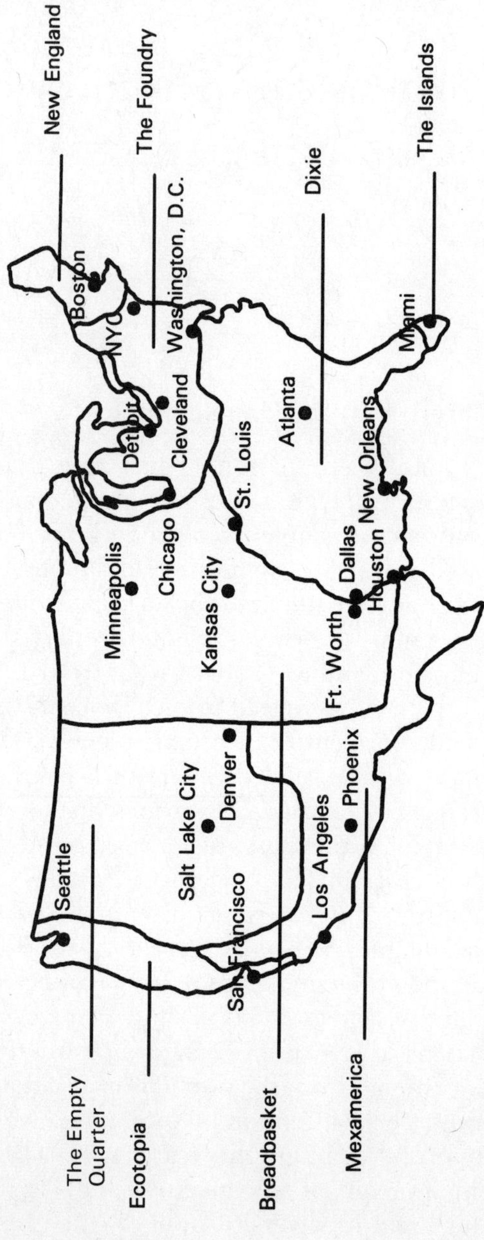

Source: Based on Garreau 1981.

Figure 5–1. *Eight Nations of the United States*

Table 5–1
Top 10 Cities with Minorities as Majorities

	% Minority, 1970	*% Minority, 1980*
East Los Angeles, Calif.	88	96
Miami, Fla.	66	81
Newark, N.J.	66	78
Gary, Ind.	60	78
Hialeah, Fla.	44	76
Washington, D.C.	73	74
Honolulu, Hawaii	68	73
Atlanta, Ga.	52	68
El Paso, Tex.	55	67
Detroit, Mich.	46	67

Source: Kasarda 1984.

point up the widespread ancestral and cultural background of U.S. citizens. Though 31 percent of U.S. citizens report a multiple ancestry, an overwhelming predominance of English, German, and Irish ancestry exists. In considering single ancestries, they account for 139 million people and are followed by 33 million people of French, Italian, and Polish descent. Five other nationalities have over one million persons each, and citizens of other than European ancestries have grown, underscoring the description of the United States as a vast market comprised of many racial segments. (Data refer to people reporting at least one ancestry; thus, persons may be included in more than one of these groups.)

The Black Population

Whites are the predominant racial segment of the U.S. population by far, as figure 5–2 indicates, making up 83.1 percent of the total. Blacks are the next largest segment and in 1980, they were 11.7 percent of the population. As a group they are nearly twice as large as the official count of the Spanish-origin group, who made up 6.4

Table 5–2
Selected U.S. (Single) Ancestry Groups: 1980

Ancestry	*Number*
Dutch	1,404,794
English	23,748,772
French	3,068,907
German	17,943,485
Greek	615,882
Hungarian	727,223
Irish	10,337,353
Italian	6,883,320
Norwegian	1,260,997
Polish	3,805,740
Portuguese	616,362
Russian	1,378,446
Scottish	1,172,904
Swedish	1,288,341
Ukranian	381,084
Other	43,931,068
Total single ancestry	118,564,678
Total, United States	226,545,805

Source: Bureau of the Census 1983c, pp. 172–81.

percent of the population. The rest of the racial minorities, such as American Indians, Eskimos and Aleuts, and Asians and Pacific Islanders, represent much smaller groups.

The black population grew from 22.6 million in 1970 to 26.5 million in 1980, an increase of 17 percent, a rate significantly higher than that of the population at large. And future estimates, until 2000, are that they will continue to grow faster, both proportionately and absolutely, than the total population. Data in table 5–3 indicate that by the year 2000 blacks will total 35,795,000, or 13.4 percent of the population—almost 1.5 times the 1985 population of Canada.

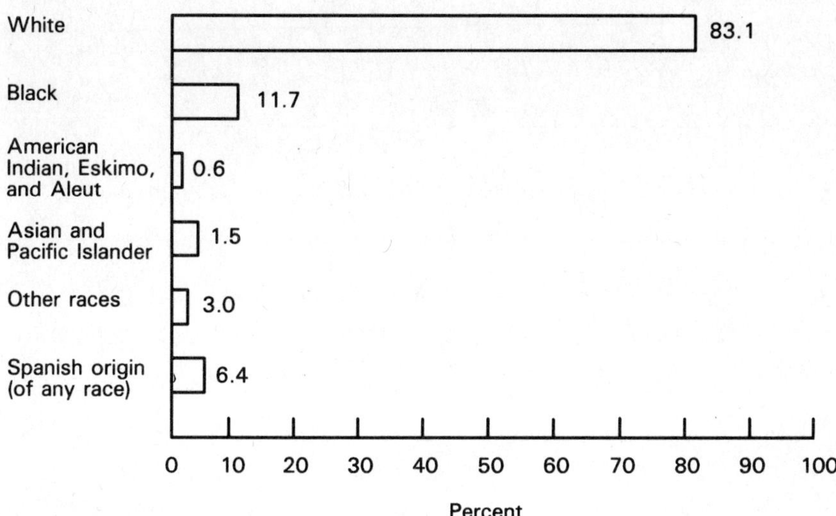

Source: Bureau of the Census 1983c, p. 1–12.

Figure 5–2. *Percentage Distribution of the Population by Race and Spanish Origin: 1980*

Black Births and Life Expectancy

Overall, the level of childbearing has been higher among black women at all ages compared with white women, as is seen in figure 5–3. The greatest differentials occur at the younger ages, among 18- and 19-year-olds. Black women, on the average, have about 50 percent more births than white women and their lifetime birth expectations exceed those of white women.

An increasing proportion of black births is occurring among unmarried women—55 percent of the births in 1982 versus 38 percent in 1970. Yet, the fertility rate of blacks, like that of their white counterparts, has also dropped significantly, from 3.1 births per woman in 1970 to 2.8 in 1980.

The life expectancy for both black males and females is increasing but on the average, whites can expect to live about 4 years longer. The 8-year life expectancy differential that exists between white males and females also exists for blacks. The average life ex-

Table 5–3
Projection of Population by Race: 1985–2000
(thousands)

		White		*Black and Other Races*		*Black*	
	Population	*Total*	*%*	*Total*	*%*	*Total*	*%*
1985	238,648	203,237	85.2	35,411	14.8	29,107	12.2
1990	249,731	210,961	84.5	38,767	15.5	31,452	12.6
1995	259,631	217,587	83.8	42,044	16.2	33,693	13.0
2000	267,990	222,801	83.1	45,189	16.9	35,795	13.4

Source: Bureau of the Census 1984.

pectancy for black males in 1981 was 66 years compared with 75 years for black females.

Geographic Concentration of Blacks

In 1980, blacks made up more than 20 percent of the population in 7 Southern states, as is shown in table 5–4. They accounted for 35 percent of Mississippi's population, 30 percent of South Carolina's, and 29 percent of Louisiana's. Twelve states had a million or more blacks representing large concentrated market potentials.

In 1980, New York had the largest number of blacks, with 1,784,337. New York was followed by Chicago with 1,197,000; Detroit, 758,939; Philadelphia, 638,878; and Los Angeles, 505,210. But on a percentage basis, East St. Louis, Illinois, ranked first, with 96 percent of its population being black, followed by Washington, D. C., with 70 percent.

Table 5–5 shows blacks as a proportion of the population in the 10 cities with the largest black population, in descending order of number. It should be noted that the undercount of the black population in the 1980 census results in understated totals.

Prior to 1970 there was an extensive migration of blacks from the South to the North. That migration, however, seems to have ended and in 1980, 53 percent of all blacks lived in the South, the same proportion as in 1970.

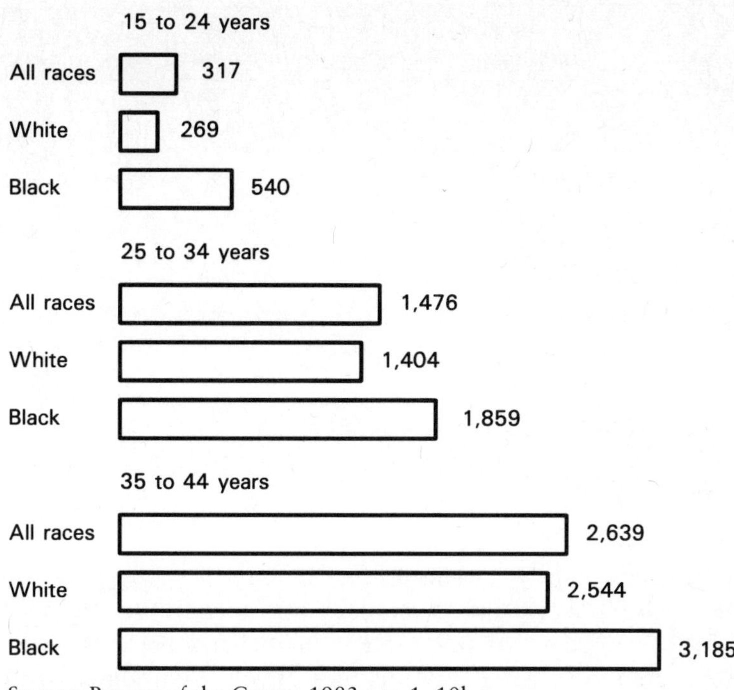

Source: Bureau of the Census 1983c, p. 1–10h.

Figure 5–3. *Children Ever Born per 1,000 Women by Age and Race: 1980 (thousands)*

Blacks are concentrated in central cities, and the proportion of the black population living there increased from about 47 percent in 1970 to 60 percent in 1980. Conversely, blacks made up only 6 percent of the total population outside of the central cities. But, as figure 5–4 indicates, like other groups, they too are moving outside central cities. In 1970, 60 percent of blacks lived in central cities; that number had declined to 57.8 percent in 1980. Those living outside central cities increased from 19.2 percent to 23.3 percent.

Black Incomes

The incomes of blacks, both as individuals and as families, generally lag behind those of their white counterparts. Data on black versus

Table 5–4
Blacks as a Percentage of the Population

State	*% of the Population*
Mississippi	35
South Carolina	30
Louisiana	29
Georgia	27
Alabama	26
Maryland	23
North Carolina	22

Source: Bureau of the Census 1983b, p. 1.

white median family income for 1971 and 1981 are presented in figure 5–5. On a relative basis, black married-couple families have realized an increase of 6.9 percent in real income from 1971 to 1981, a time when the real incomes of white families hardly increased at all. As for individuals, the income of black males with college degrees is now about the same as that of their white counterparts. But the comparison for black females is not the same.

The 1979 median income for households of various races is given in figure 5–6. The disparity between all households and white households is not great. The median income of all households was about 95 percent that of white households. Nevertheless, black families have not fared well, as their median income is only about 60 percent that of white families. This reflects an increasing proportion of black families being maintained by females with no husband present. Black women in 1980 had average earnings of 74 percent of black men's earnings; the white woman–man ratio in 1980 was about 60 percent.

Comparing 1970 with 1980 the number of black families below the poverty level increased by 1 million from 8 to 9 million. Most of the increase was among families maintained by women. Overall, the high proportion of all black families below the poverty level remained about the same for both 1970 and 1980—34 percent.

Table 5–5
Ten Cities with the Largest Black Population by Rank: 1980

Rank	City	Black Population: Number	Black Population: % of Total	Total Population
	United States	26,495,025	11.7	226,545,805
1.	New York, N.Y.	1,784,337	25.2	7,071,639
2.	Chicago, Ill.	1,197,000	39.8	3,005,072
3.	Detroit, Mich.	758,939	63.1	1,203,339
4.	Philadelphia, Pa.	638,878	37.8	1,688,210
5.	Los Angeles, Calif.	505,210	17.0	2,966,850
6.	Washington, D.C.	448,906	70.3	638,333
7.	Houston, Tex.	440,346	27.6	1,595,138
8.	Baltimore, Md.	431,151	54.8	786,775
9.	New Orleans, La.	308,149	55.3	557,515
10.	Memphis, Tenn.	307,702	47.6	646,356

Source: Bureau of the Census 1983b, p. 2.

[a]East St. Louis, Ill., exceeds Washington, D.C., in percentage of blacks in population: 96 percent.

Black Families and Households

Figure 5–7 deals with marital status and shows that blacks have different patterns than whites or Hispanics. Data on black families by type for 1970 and 1982 are given in figures 5–8 and 5–9. They highlight the different family makeups, and an increase in the proportion of black female householder families from 28 to 40 percent, and a decrease in married couple families from 68 to 55 percent since 1970.

The importance of the black mother's family and decision-making role is underlined by the data. Black women are more likely to be family householders than are white women, and have a higher proportion of children under 18. An estimated three-fourths of black children born in the 1970s will spend some time living with the mother only.

Of the 4.9 million black families in 1970, 68 percent were maintained by married couples and 28 percent by women. By 1982, however, although the number of black families had increased by 30 percent to 6.4 million, the proportion of families maintained by women grew by about 50 percent, reaching 41 percent of all black

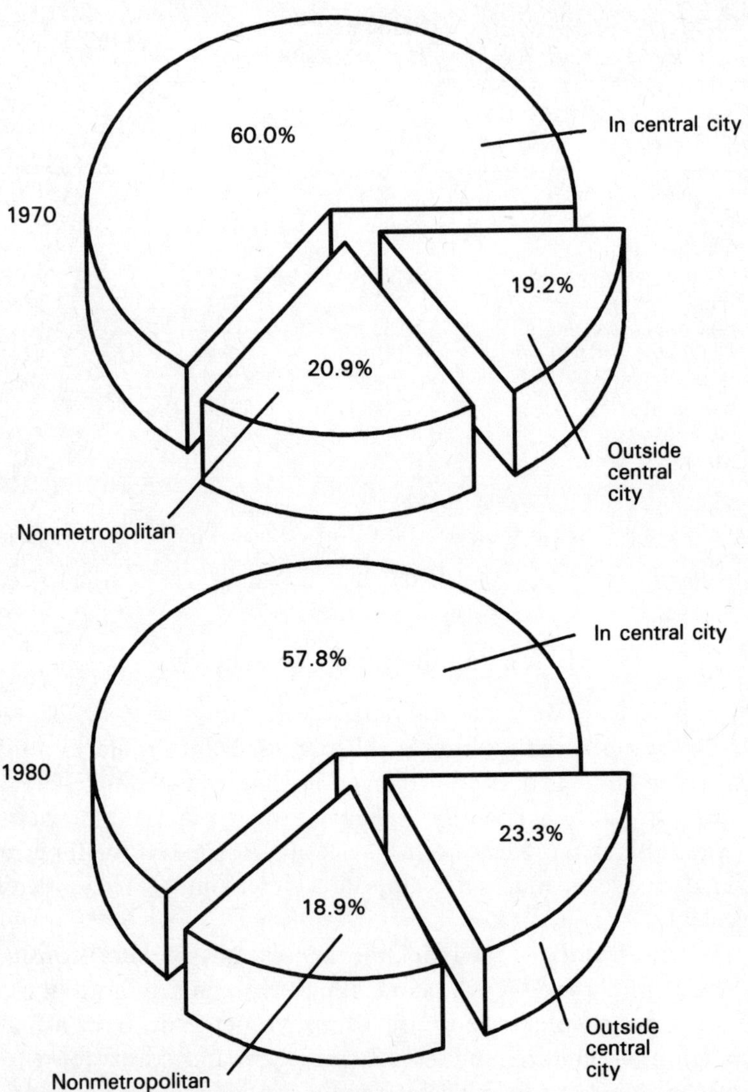

Source: Bureau of the Census 1983b, p. 5.

Figure 5–4. *Residential Local of Black Population, 1970–1980*

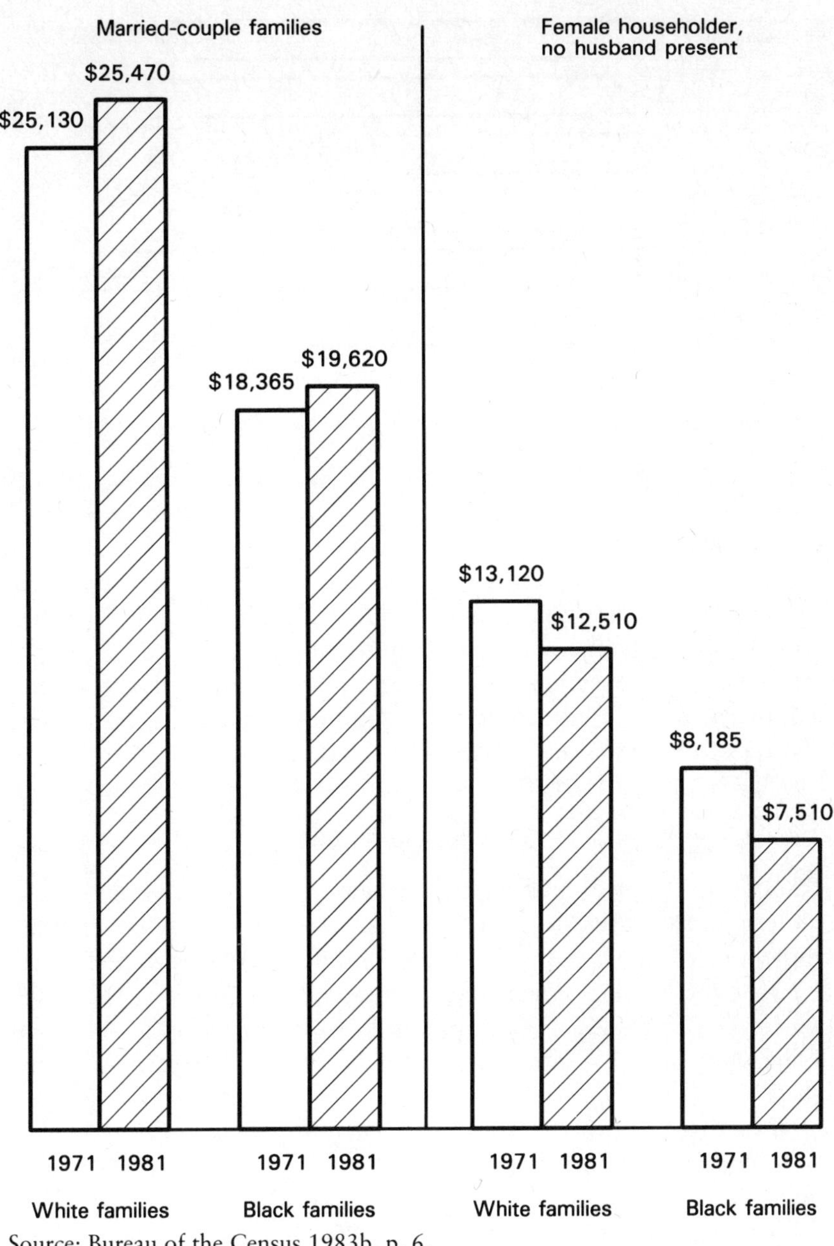

Source: Bureau of the Census 1983b, p. 6.

Figure 5–5. *Median Family Income by Type of Family and Race of Householder: 1971 and 1981 (1981 dollars)*

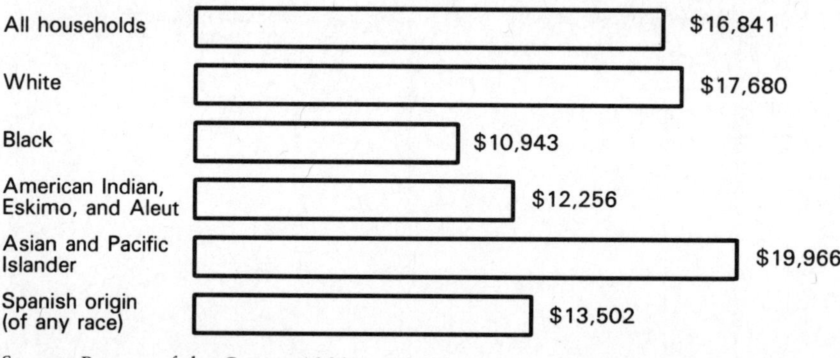

Source: Bureau of the Census 1983c, p. 1–10t.

Figure 5–6. *Median Income in 1979 for Selected Population Groups*

households. Conversely, those black families maintained by married couples fell to 55 percent. Though a majority of black families is still maintained by married couples, about one-third of the black women who maintained families had never married, while 37.8 percent of black families are female householder families. The trend raises the question whether the proportion of single black families will overtake married-couple black families in the near future. The market implications are worthy of consideration.

Black Single Parents

The importance of black women in families as breadwinners, consumers, and household decision makers relative to white women and those of Spanish origin is quite pointed. Approximately one-third of the black women that maintained families in 1982 never married. As a result, the number and proportion of black children living with both parents decreased from 68 to 51 percent between 1970 and 1982.

The divorce ratio (the ratio of currently divorced persons to 1,000 married persons living with spouses) is the highest for blacks when compared with whites and Hispanics. The ratio for black women was 265/1,000 versus 128/1,000 for white women. The combined divorce ratio for black men and women in 1982 was 220/1,000; for white men and women it was 107/1,000. The data sug-

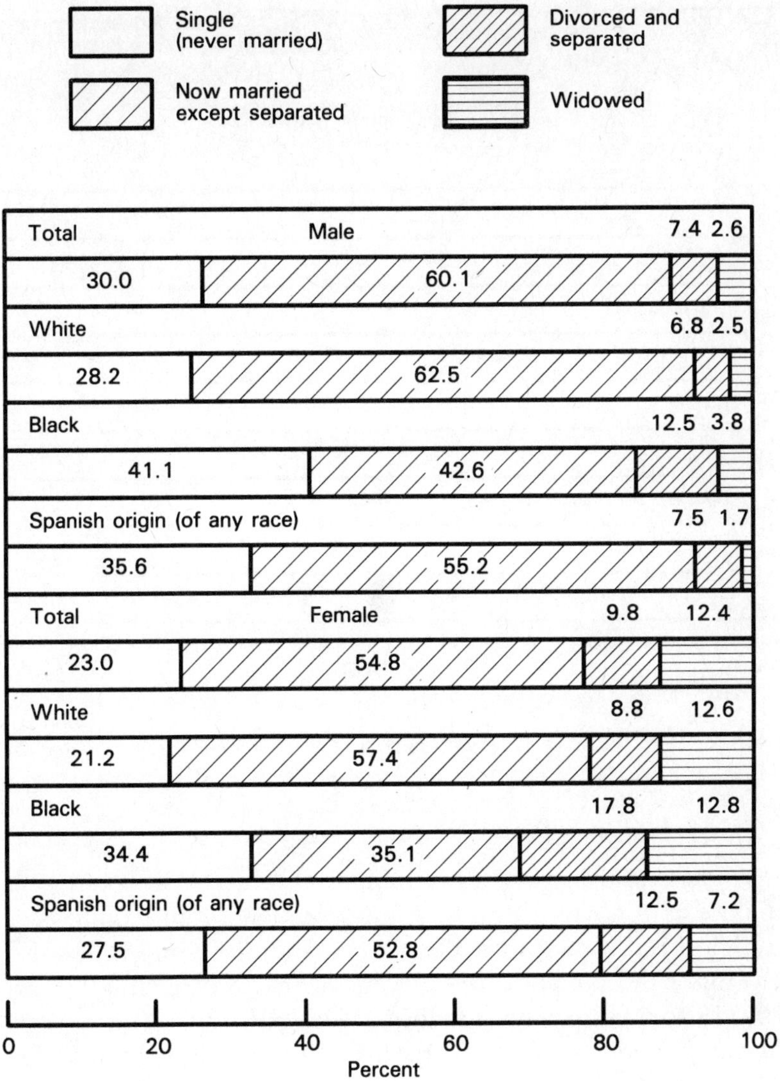

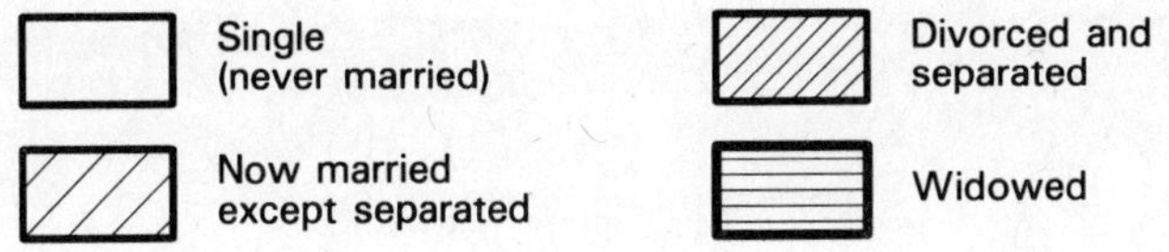

Source: Bureau of the Census 1981, p. 1–15.

Figure 5–7. *Marital Status of Persons 15 Years and Over by Sex, Race, and Spanish Origin: 1980*

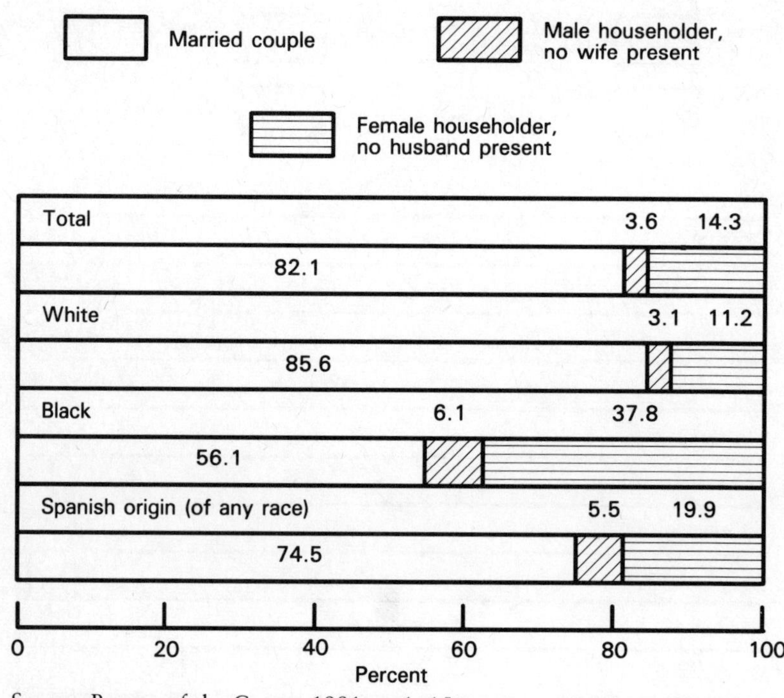

Source: Bureau of the Census 1981, p. 1–15.

Figure 5–8. *Family Type as a Percentage of All Families by Race and Spanish Origin: 1980*

gest a potential for greater instability and insecurity among black families as compared with white and Spanish-origin families.

The black home ownership occupancy rate in 1980 was just two-thirds that of whites, 44 percent versus 68 percent. Proportionately, black home ownership increased significantly over the 1970–80 decade with a 45 percent growth from 2.6 million to 3.7 million. This suggests the possibility of a burgeoning housing market as blacks move up the income ladder.

Black Education and Labor-force Participation

Education is a key to increasing incomes, improving life-styles, and hence, to growing market opportunities. Blacks still lag behind

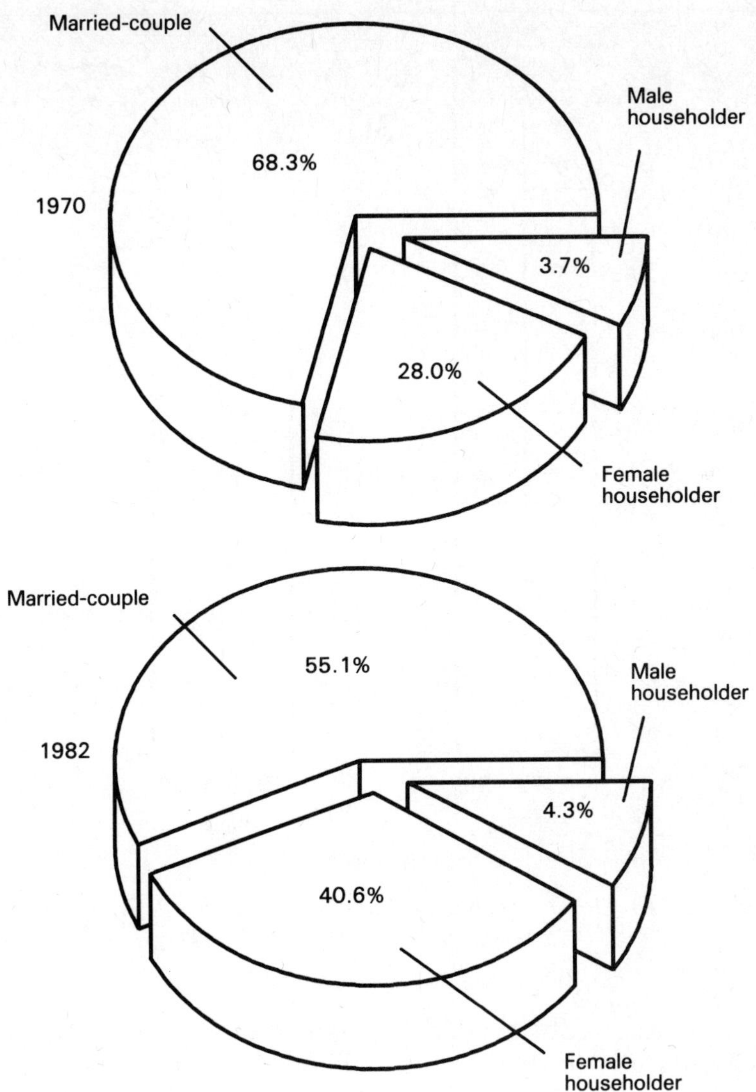

Source: Bureau of the Census 1983b, p. 9.

Figure 5–9. *Black Families by Type: 1970 and 1982*

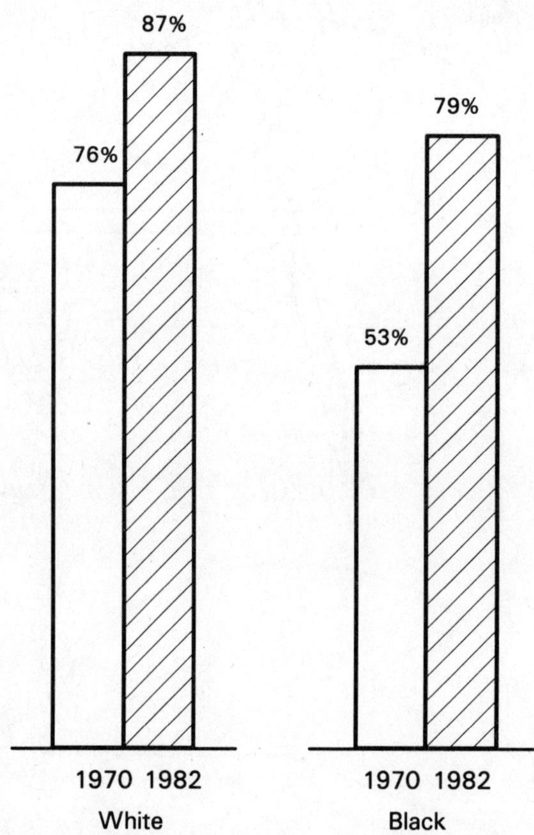

Source: Bureau of the Census 1983b, p. 17.

Figure 5–10. *Percentage High School Graduates for Persons 25 to 34 Years Old by Race: 1970 and 1982*

whites educationally, although substantial progress is being made to close the gap. In 1981, about 1 million blacks, aged 18–34, were in college, double the number in 1970. As a proportion of the total college population, blacks grew from just 7 percent in 1970 to 11 percent in 1981. The percentage of black high school graduates among 25–34-year-olds has increased by 50 percent from 1970 to 1982, as is shown in figure 5–10.

In 1982, blacks comprised about 10 percent of the civilian labor force, totaling 11 million. They had a large increase in the decade 1972 to 1982 as their labor-force participation increased by 2.7 million, or 31 percent. The number of unemployed blacks, however, increased even faster, by 140 percent. This increase of 1.3 million in unemployment resulted in the highest unemployment rate since World War II, 18.9 percent. The rate is double the unemployment rate for whites, and the 1982 unemployment rate for black teenagers was a horrendous 48 percent. Blacks suffer from the last-hired-and-first-fired syndrome.

As compared with whites, blacks' employment patterns are far different. Black workers are concentrated in 3 occupational groupings: operators, fabricators, and laborers, 27 percent; technical sales and administrative support, 24 percent; and services, 23 percent. They are underrepresented in the higher-paying managerial and professional groups, which account for but 13 percent of black workers. Farming, forestry, and fishing account for a mere 2 percent.

The Hispanic Population

Americans of Spanish origin are such a diverse group that there is no agreement on who should be included in that category. In addition, hard data on the total number of Hispanics do not exist because of the significant number of undocumented Hispanic aliens, or illegals, who live in the United States. The majority of Hispanics are recent immigrants who maintain their culture. They are an identifiable market but an unidentifiable group with market demands that vary somewhat from those of other U.S. markets.

For this discussion we shall use the census definitions and data, and the terms "Spanish," "Spanish origin," and "Hispanics" will be used interchangeably. Cubans, Mexicans, Puerto Ricans, and people from South and Central America, as well as those indicating they were of other Spanish/Hispanic origin, are included. We shall assume that an estimated 2.5–5 million Hispanics entered the United States illegally over the 1970–80 decade alone, although the actual figure may well be higher.

Hard data on the actual number of Hispanics in the United

Table 5–6
People of Spanish Origin

	1970		*1980*	
	Number	*%*	*Number*	*%*
Mexican	4,532,435	50	8,678,632	60
Puerto Rican	1,004,961	16	1,429,396	14
Cuban	544,600	6	806,223	6
Other Spanish	2,566,171	28	3,113,867	20
Total	9,072,602	100	14,603,683	100

Source: Bureau of the Census 1985.

States are difficult to derive, but table 5–6 deals with people of Spanish origin using 1980 census data. The recorded total was 14,603,683. An independent postcensus estimate in March 1982 resulted in a figure of 15.4 million Hispanics, but the 1980 data were used as a base for this (Bureau of the Census 1982). If this 15 million figure is coupled with an estimated 2.5–5 million undocumented aliens in the 1970–80 decade, estimates of over 20 million Hispanics are derived. And, indeed, those of Spanish origin could well rival blacks as the largest U.S. minority shortly after the turn of the century.

In actual numbers, though every Spanish group grew over the 1970–80 decade, only the number of Mexicans increased relatively, growing from 50 percent in 1970 to 60 percent of the 1980 total Hispanic population. The situation for the remaining segments was: other Spanish, which in 1970 included 17 percent from Central and South America, fell from 28 to 20 percent; Cubans, who totaled 6 percent, remained the same but made up a most important income and education component; the 16-percent Puerto Rican group fell to 14 percent.

Overall, the recorded Hispanic population grew from an estimated 4.5 percent of the total population in 1970 to 6.4 percent in 1980, and some projections are that it will reach 11.3 percent by 2000, when Hispanics will start to rival blacks as the dominant U.S. minority. Currently, Hispanic households represent a substantial and growing market segment with aggregate 1983 after-tax estimates of buying power of about $70 billion (Bureau of the Census 1983a).

The total Hispanic population may account for one-fourth of the nation's growth over the next 20 years. It is projected to grow three times faster than the U.S. total, with the present estimated share of 7 percent of the total population rising to 12 percent by 2020 and 16 percent by 2050. The 1986 estimated Hispanic total of 17.3 million is projected to reach 36.5 million in 2020 and 51 million in 2050.

Hispanics: Childbearing

In 1982, the childbearing rates of Spanish origin women 18–34 years old was higher than that of women at large and about the same as that for black women. Spanish married women 15–44 years old had on the average proportionately more children born per woman and proportionately fewer childless women than the non-Hispanic population. For Hispanic women the average number of children ever born was 1.6 compared with 1.3 for non-Hispanic women. Hispanic families averaged 3.89 people compared with 3.22 for non-Hispanics (Bureau of the Census 1982). The proportion of Hispanic families with 5 or more children in 1982 was 30 percent versus 16 percent for the total population. Yet, like all families, the average size of the Hispanic family is falling and was lower in 1982 than it was in 1970.

Hispanics: Age

Except for Cubans, Spanish origin people are decidedly younger than both the population at large and those not of Spanish origin. Figure 5–11 gives the age distribution based on 1980 census data by types of Spanish origin. The 1980 median age was 22 years versus 31 years for the population at large—a significant difference (Bureau of the Census 1982). The 1982 estimate increases the median age to 23.7 years, still relatively low. Mexican and Puerto Rican Hispanics have a median age of only 22 years, but the Cuban Hispanics are much older. Their median age is 38.1 years (Census 1983c).

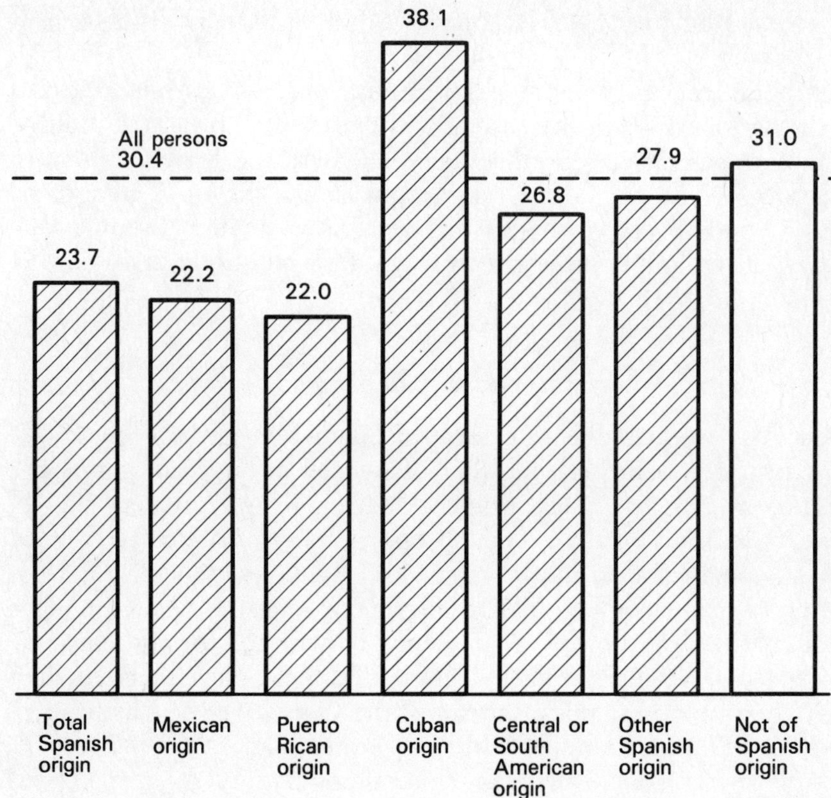

Source: Bureau of the Census 1982, p. 3.

Figure 5–11. *Median Age of All Persons and Persons of Spanish Origin, by Type of Spanish Origin: March 1982*

The age differences of Hispanics are noticeable at both ends of the age spectrum. About 12 percent were under 5 years old in 1980 versus just 7 percent for the total population. At the other extreme, just 5 percent are 65 and over versus 11 percent overall.

Geographic Concentration of Hispanics

Of the estimated 14.6 million plus Hispanics in 1980, 8.8 million were concentrated in 5 Southwestern states with two states, Cali-

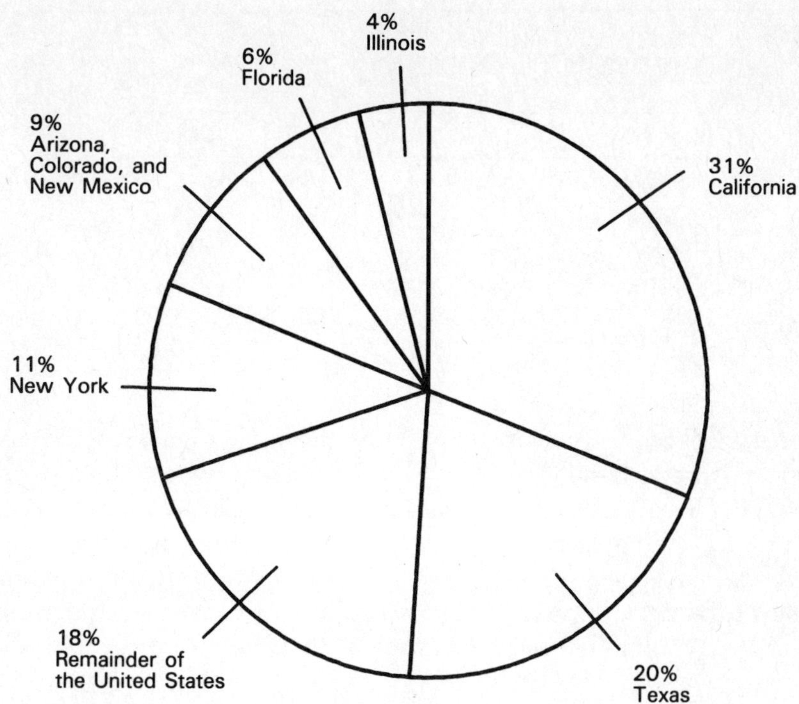

Source: Bureau of the Census 1981, p. 1–14.

Figure 5–12. *Percentage Distribution of Persons of Spanish Origin by Residence in Selected States: 1980*

fornia and Texas, accounting for 7.5 million, or over 50 percent of the total, as can be seen in figure 5–12.

The number of recorded Hispanics in the top four states is shown in table 5–7. California is the leader by far and 80 percent of California's 4.5 million people of Spanish origin are of Mexican descent. Los Angeles has been referred to as the second largest Mexican city in the world after Mexico City. New York state reported 1.7 million Hispanics, about 9 percent of its total population. In New Mexico, 36.7 percent of the total population were of Spanish origin and San Antonio, Texas, has fewer non-Hispanics than Mexicans.

Outside of the Southwestern states and New York, Florida has the greatest Hispanic concentration, about 858,000, or about 9 per-

Table 5–7
Distribution of Spanish Origin by States: 1980 Census

State	*Number*
California	4,544,331
Texas	2,985,824
New York	1,659,300
Florida	858,158

Source: Bureau of the Census 1985, p. 29.

cent of its population. Most are Cubans, who have had great impact on reshaping Miami.

The 10 largest Hispanic market areas are shown in table 5–8, along with the percentage of the metropolitan population they represent. Los Angeles–Long Beach, New York, and Miami head the list. Hispanics comprise almost two-thirds of El Paso's population and close to one-half of San Antonio's total.

Hispanic Earnings and Family Income

Figures 5–13 and table 5–9 deal with incomes of Spanish origin families. The money incomes of Hispanics were substantially lower in 1981 than those for non-Hispanics. In 1981, the per-capita income for Hispanics was $5,300, versus $8,500 for all persons (Bureau of the Census 1982). The median earnings of Hispanic men was 70 percent of non-Spanish men: $10,800 versus $15,400. And for Spanish origin families the median income was $16,400 versus $22,800 for non-Hispanic families. As is shown in table 5–9, Hispanic families have a smaller proportion in the higher income categories. Their proportion of $25,000-and-over families is about 62 percent of all families, and about 61 percent of non-Hispanic families. In comparing 1981 income data by regions, the median income of Hispanic families exceeds that of blacks, except in the Northeastern region.

Of all Hispanic families, Puerto Ricans had the lowest median family income by far, realizing just 63 percent of the Cuban median,

Table 5–8
Spanish Origin as a Proportion of 10 Largest Standard Metropolitan Statistical Areas: 1980

Metropolitan Area	*Number*	*% of Metropolitan Population*
Los Angeles–Long Beach, Calif.	2,066,103	27.6
New York, N.Y.–N.J.	1,493,148	16.4
Miami, Fla.	580,994	35.7
Chicago, Ill.	580,609	8.2
San Antonio, Tex.	481,511	44.9
Houston, Tex.	424,903	14.6
San Francisco–Oakland, Calif.	351,698	10.8
El Paso, Tex.	297,001	61.9
Riverside–San Bernardino–Ontario, Calif.	290,280	18.6
Anaheim–Santa Ana–Garden Grove, Calif.	286,339	14.8

Source: Bureau of the Census 1982.

and only 69 percent of the total Spanish origin family median. Cuban family incomes exceeded those of other Hispanic groups and were followed by "other Spanish families" and Mexicans. Hispanic families overall are not as well off as the total population. Of all U.S. families, 31 percent were in the under $15,000 category, but a large proportion of each Hispanic group was included in that category. This is reflected partly in the fact that 22.7 percent of the Spanish origin families were maintained by women with no husband present, who on the average have a lower median income than married-couple families or those maintained by males with no wife present.

Although 24 percent of Spanish origin families were recorded as being below the poverty level in 1981, they comprise a smaller proportion than did blacks. In 1978, 28 percent of blacks were below the poverty level versus 20 percent of all Spanish families. Figure 5–14 indicates the number and proportion of Hispanics below the poverty level. Husband–wife Spanish families earned 2.5 times the income of families maintained by women with no husband present.

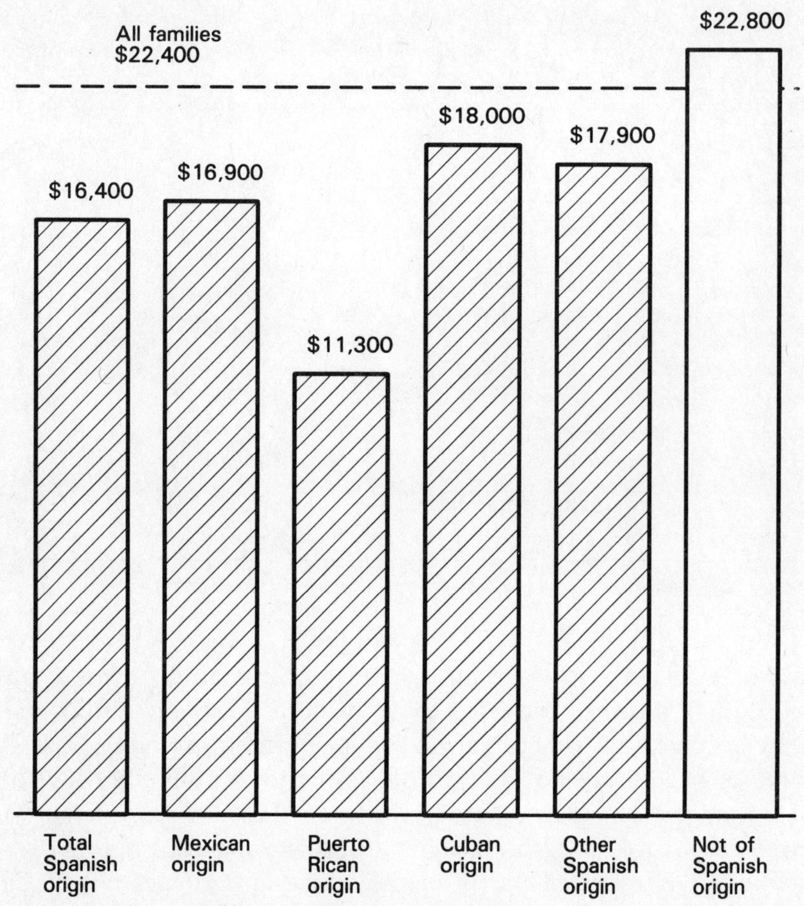

Source: Bureau of the Census 1982, p. 5.

Figure 5–13. *Median Money Income 1981 of All Families and Families of Spanish Origin, by Type of Spanish Origin*

Hispanic Families and Marital Status

As figure 5–7 indicates, the marital status of Hispanics differs considerably from that of blacks. Proportionately, compared to blacks, Hispanics have fewer females that have never married, fewer that are either divorced or separated, and far fewer that are widowed. As for the men, there are also fewer proportionately that are single, divorced and separated, or widowers.

Table 5–9

Money Income in 1981 of All Families and Spanish Origin Families: March 1982

		Spanish Origin Families					
Family Income	*Total Families*	*Total*	*Mexican*	*Puerto Rican*	*Cuban*	*Other Spanish*	*Families Not of Spanish Origin*
Total families (thousands)	61,019	3,305	1,971	486	236	613	57,714
Percent	100.0	100.0	100.0	100.0	100.0	100.0	100.0
Under $5,000	5.8	10.0	8.3	20.5	9.4	7.5	5.6
$5,000–$7,499	5.5	9.2	8.3	15.9	4.9	8.1	5.3
$7,500–$9,999	6.0	8.7	8.5	10.1	8.5	8.2	5.8
$10,000–$14,999	13.6	17.6	18.4	13.7	19.9	17.3	13.3
$15,000–$19,999	12.6	15.1	15.8	15.0	11.1	14.8	12.4
$20,000–$24,999	12.5	12.0	12.2	9.5	12.5	12.6	12.2
$25,000+	44.1	27.5	28.8	15.2	32.6	30.8	45.0
Median income	$22,388	$16,402	$16,933	$11,256	$18,009	$17,891	$22,801

Source: Bureau of the Census 1982.

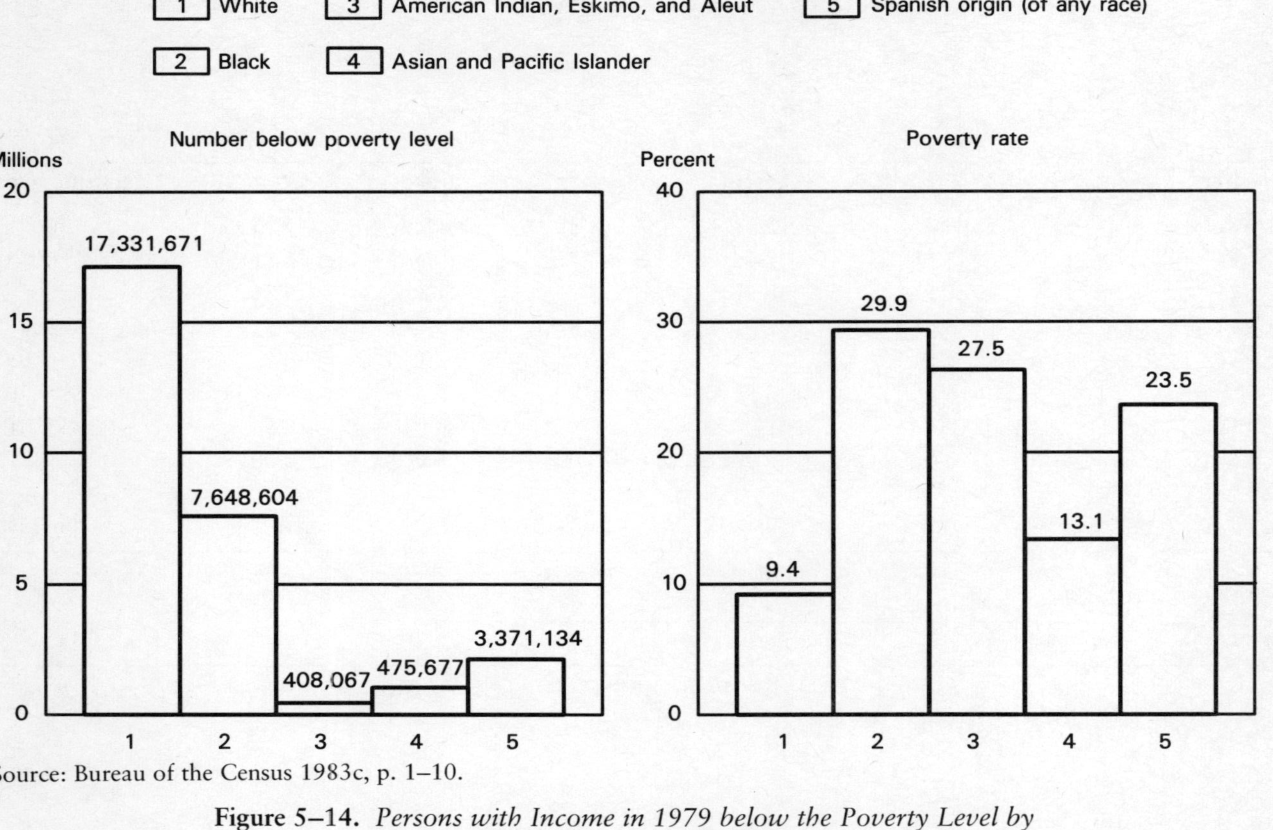

Source: Bureau of the Census 1983c, p. 1–10.

Figure 5–14. *Persons with Income in 1979 below the Poverty Level by Race and Spanish Origin*

Figure 5–8 contains 1980 data comparing Spanish origin with black families. The former have a much larger proportion of married couples and a significantly smaller proportion of female householder families.

In March 1982 there were 3.3 million Spanish origin families recorded in the United States, and 2.4 million were married-couple families (Bureau of the Census 1985). Almost all of the 5.4 million children under 18 years of age lived within families and a striking 69 percent lived with both parents. 25 percent lived with the mother only while 2 percent lived with the father only (Bureau of the Census 1984b, p. 4). Spanish origin families are more likely to live in metropolitan areas in the central cities than non-Spanish families.

In 1985, 23 percent of the Spanish families were maintained by women with no husband present, roughly one-half the proportion for blacks (44 percent) (Taeuber & Valdisera 1986, p. 9). The larger Spanish families, coupled with lower family incomes than those of other families, contribute to lower per-capita income and disposable household incomes. Spanish people tend to marry at younger ages than do non-Spanish. And a disparity exists among the proportion of single and never-married men and women 15 years and older: 34.2 percent for men versus 25.5 percent for women. Interestingly, almost twice as many Spanish women reported they were divorced as men. Speculations about reasons for this include the hypotheses that these women might be spurred by rising education levels and employment opportunities. Should this be so, it could portend a greater number of divorces among Hispanic families in the future as female educational levels and employment opportunities rise. But this need not necessarily follow.

Some researchers suggest that there seem to be two kinds of Spanish origin families in the United States. First, there are those steeped in Spanish tradition and culture, who are seeking to maintain their Spanish ways and identities. Second, there are those families, particularly the younger families, who like previous migrants, seek to become rapidly integrated into the U.S. mainstream. Yet, at the same time, the latter still maintain much of their "ethnicity" in the form of various Hispanic traditions and values. Both kinds of families continue to have an impact on U.S. culture, tastes, and values, particularly in the Southwestern states.

Hispanic Employment and Education

In 1984, persons 16 years old and over of Spanish origin had a higher average unemployment rate than the population at large, 11.6 percent versus 7.5 percent respectively, but not as high as that of blacks, 15.9 percent (Bureau of the Census 1984b). Table 5–10 deals with 1982 Spanish origin employment status and occupation groups. Their occupational characteristics are quite different than those of the population at large: only 6.3 percent of the Spanish employed labor force are managers and administrators (excluding farm) versus 11.7 percent for the general population (Bureau of the Census 1982a). Hispanics only have about one-half the proportion of professional, technical, and kindred workers, 8.8 percent versus 17.2 percent. A relatively large proportion, 23.2 percent, are operatives, versus 13.2 percent for the total population.

People of Hispanic origin significantly lag behind the total population in education, which is reflected in lower incomes and job categories. In 1982, only 46 percent of all Hispanics 25 years old and over had completed high school versus about 72 percent of the non-Spanish origin population (Bureau of the Census 1982). More than twice the proportion of non-Spanish persons versus Spanish persons completed 4 years of college—18 percent versus 8 percent. The educational gap between Hispanics and non-Hispanics 25 years old and over remains, but the educational attainment of young Hispanics is increasing. Also, educational attainment varies by Spanish origin categories. In general, persons reporting in the Central and South American and "other Spanish" categories have higher levels of educational attainment and Mexicans the lowest. Of those 25 and over in 1982, 50 percent of Cubans, 42 percent of Puerto Ricans and 41 percent of Mexicans completed 4 years or more of high school.

Summary

The United States is a nation within nations made up of widely diverse racial and cultural backgrounds. An overwhelming majority of those reporting single ancestry, 139 million, are of English, Ger-

Table 5–10

Hispanic Employment Status and Major Occupation Groups, Both Sexes: March 1982

Employment Status and Occupation	*Total Population*	*Spanish Origin*					*Not of Spanish Origin*
		Total	*Mexican*	*Puerto Rican*	*Cuban*	*Other*	
Persons 16 years old and over (thousands)	172,537	9,257	5,578	1,213	703	1,762	163,280
In civilian labor force (thousands)	108,762	5,916	3,702	623	427	1,164	102,845
% unemployed	9.7	13.4	13.3	17.3	10.8	12.4	9.5
Employed (thousands)	98,208	5,124	3,208	516	381	1,020	93,084
%	100.0	100.0	100.0	100.0	100.0	100.0	100.0
Professional, technical, and kindred workers	17.2	8.8	6.8	8.6	15.2	12.7	17.7
Managers and administrators, except farm	11.7	6.3	5.9	3.9	7.7	8.2	12.0
Sales workers	6.6	4.1	3.6	4.2	6.5	4.8	6.7
Clerical and kindred workers	18.4	17.4	15.8	24.6	18.0	18.4	18.5
Craft and kindred workers	12.4	13.2	14.5	10.6	13.0	10.6	12.3
Operatives, including transport	13.2	23.2	23.7	26.9	23.8	19.6	12.6
Operatives, except transport	9.8	19.0	19.5	21.6	20.0	16.0	9.3
Transport equipment operatives	3.4	4.2	4.3	5.3	3.8	3.5	3.4
Laborers, excluding farm	4.2	6.8	8.3	3.8	4.6	4.2	4.1
Farmers and farm managers	1.4	0.1	0.1	—	—	0.4	1.4
Farm laborers and supervisors	1.0	3.0	4.7	0.2	—	0.2	0.9
Service workers	13.0	17.1	16.5	17.2	11.2	20.9	13.7

Source: Bureau of the Census 1982, p. 24.

man, and Irish ancestry. Yet, minorities are important for they are reported to comprise the majority in 25 cities of 100,000 or more in population. Two minority groups stand out, blacks and those of Spanish origin.

Blacks made up 11.7 percent of the population in 1980 while the official count of Hispanics was 6.4 percent. Numerically, other minority groups, such as Asians and Pacific Islanders, Eskimos, Aleuts, and Indians, are quite small.

The black population in the 1970s grew by 4 million, a rate significantly higher than that of the general population. By 2000 they are projected to total almost 36 million, over 13 percent of our population.

Black women have more births and higher lifetime birth expectations than white women. Unmarried women accounted for 55 percent of births in 1982. The life expectancy for blacks is about 4 years lower than it is for whites.

In 1980, blacks made up more than 20 percent of the population in 7 Southern states, accounting for 35 percent of Mississippi's population. New York City had the largest black concentration. The pre-1970 migration from the South to the North now seems to have ended, and although blacks are starting to move outside central cities, 60 percent of blacks still live in central cities.

Incomes of blacks, both of individuals and families, lag behind those of their white counterparts. Relatively, black households realized a net gain in the 1970s. The median income of all households is 95 percent that of white households, but the median income of black families is only 60 percent that of white families. This reflects the large proportion of families maintained by black women with no male present as well as a higher proportion of single black male households. Blacks have a higher proportion of divorced, separated, or widowed women than do Hispanics or whites.

Blacks have a higher proportion of singles, both males and females 15 and over, than do whites and Hispanics. They have a greater proportion of divorced males. Of black families, 37.8 percent are female householder families; black couples make up but 56 percent of families. About one-third of black women who maintained families in 1982 had never married, and the divorce ratio for married black women is higher than it is for white women. From 1970 to 1982 the proportion of black female householder families grew from 28 to 40 percent, while married couple families declined from 68 to 55 percent. The divorce ratio for blacks is higher when compared to whites or Hispanics. The importance of the black mother in the family and her decision-making role is understood.

Blacks still lag behind whites educationally although the gap is closing. They grew as a proportion of the total college population from 7 percent in 1970 to 11 percent in 1981. Their unemployment rate is double that of whites and the employed are concentrated in 3 occupational groupings.

Hispanics comprise a diverse group including Cubans, Mexicans, Puerto Ricans, and people from Central and South America. Because of the large number of illegal immigrants, hard data are difficult to obtain. The official estimates of Hispanics range from 14.6 to 15.4 million, from 4.5 to 6.4 percent of the population between 1970 and 1980. Allowing for the millions of illegal immigrants, a total of perhaps over 20 million Hispanics does not seem out of line. After the year 2000 Hispanics could rival the numbers and power of blacks.

Between 1970 and 1980, while all Hispanic origin groups grew, only the Mexicans gained relatively, growing from 50 percent to 60 percent of the total. The proportion of Hispanics from Central and South America fell.

In 1982, Spanish origin women 18–34 years old had higher childbearing and fertility rates than did women at large. Their families are substantially larger than are non-Spanish families, averaging 3.89 people compared with 3.22 for non-Hispanics. Even so, the average size of Hispanic families has been falling.

Those of Spanish origin, except for Cubans, are decidedly younger than the population at large, with a median age of 22 versus 31 years, even though the Cuban segment's median age is 38.1 years. As was noted previously, Hispanics have a higher proportion of children under 5 than the total population, and fewer 65 and over.

About 60 percent of all Hispanics are concentrated in 5 Southwestern states with California and Texas accounting for over 50 percent of the total. California is the leading state and Los Angeles is reputed to be the second largest Mexican city in the world. Hispanics are 36.7 percent of the total population of New Mexico; San Antonio has fewer non-Hispanics than Mexicans.

The per-capita earnings of Hispanics are lower than those for non-Hispanics, $5,300 versus $8,500. In 1981, Hispanic families had a median income of $16,400, compared to $22,800 for non-Hispanic families. Hispanic men only earned 70 percent of non-Hispanic men, Hispanic families earned significantly less and had a smaller proportion in the higher income categories than non-Hispanic families. Their median income in 1981 was $16,400 versus $22,800 for non-Hispanic families. Puerto Rican families had the lowest median family incomes and Cubans had the highest. As compared with black families a much smaller proportion of Hispanic families is below the poverty level.

Hispanic educational levels are not as high as the general population with 62 percent having less than a high school education.

As compared with blacks, Hispanics had fewer females that have never married, a larger proportion of married-couple families, fewer separated and divorced, larger-sized families, and a more traditional family and childbearing role for women.

Almost all Hispanic children in 1982 lived within families, with 69 percent of all children under 18 living with both parents. As compared with blacks, proportionately, about one-half the Hispanic families are maintained by women. Large families coupled with lower incomes results in lower per-capita incomes than is the case for the population at large.

Both Spanish origin men and women have higher unemployment rates than the general population does, but their rates are not as high as those for blacks. Their occupations are also different, with proportionately more operatives, and fewer professionals, managers, and administrators. Though they lag behind the population in education (with those reporting as Central and South American and "other Spanish" having the highest attainment and the Mexicans the lowest) nevertheless the educational levels of the young Hispanics in total is increasing.

References

Bureau of the Census. 1981. *1980 Census of Population: General Population Characteristics*. Vol. 1 PC 80-1.

———. 1982. *Persons of Spanish Origin in the United States: March 1982*. Series P-20, no. 396.

———. 1983a. *After-Tax Money Income Estimates of Households: 1983*.

———. 1983b. *America's Black Population: 1970 to 1982*. Special Publication P-10/Pop 83-1.

———. 1983c. *1980 Census of Population: General and Social Economic Characteristics*. Vol. 1 (December).

———. 1984a. *Marital Status and Living Arrangements: March 1983*. Series P-20, no. 389 (July).

———. 1984b. *Projections of the Population of the United States by Age, Sex, and Race: 1983 to 2080*. Series P-25, no. 952.

———. 1985. *Statistical Abstract of the United States: 1986*. 106th ed.

Bureau of Labor Statistics. 1983. *Women at Work: A Chartbook*. Bulletin 168 (April).

Garreau, Joel. 1981. *The Nine Nations of North America*. Boston: Houghton Mifflin.

Kasarda, John D. 1984. "Hispanics and City Change." *American Demographics* (November):25–30.

Taeuber, Cynthia M., and Victor Valdisera. 1986. "Women in the American Economy." Bureau of the Census. Series P-23, no. 146 (November).

6
Working Women: Market Implications

The Changing Scene

The most dramatic socioeconomic change since the mid-1960s has been the growing proportion of working women, particularly working wives and mothers. It has transformed markets, products, families, homes, workplace conditions, and indeed, our fundamental life-styles. It has pushed our economy in new directions and opened up many new market opportunities.

The executive president of a food conglomerate, commenting recently at a marketing conference, noted that "working wives have affected our industry as much as any other factor." They have influenced the family meal scene, the fast-food industry, prepared foods in supermarkets, household services, store and restaurant hours, and the mechanization of household duties. They add to the family's discretionary income but also create a poverty of time, less time to shop and perform other tasks.

As a result of women's labor-force participation, the roles of family members have shifted. An increased standard of living has resulted because wives, on the average, add 18 percent to the family income. Also, with the prospect of two retirement pensions, husband–wife families are more willing to spend now because they expect to realize more substantial retirement benefits than their predecessors.

In the 1950s and early 1960s, the concept of gainfully employed women, particularly working wives, was not well accepted. Social and cultural conventions worked against the concept. It was quite acceptable for married women to engage in volunteer work for non-profit organizations such as opera companies, symphony orchestras, hospitals, and other charitable and/or religious organizations, but working for pay cast aspersions on the family, particularly the husband. It was usually construed as an indication that the husband was not able to support his wife and family. The in-laws became concerned and the statement that "she had to go to work" was an unflattering one. Now, however, if a woman works outside the home she is realizing and fulfilling herself, she is utilizing her capabilities and skills, and is benefiting the family economically, and has an understanding family.

There has been a major change in the past 25 years. The growing acceptance of working women results from such factors as the feminist movement, changing educational and workplace opportunities for women, and the rising costs of maintaining a family.

Females in the Population

Figure 6–1, the age and sex population triangle, shows the male and female population distribution. In it the 1970 and 1980 population are broken down by age groups with females on the right side of the triangle and males on the left. What is most noticeable is that the overall shape of the distribution of females and males is similar, with an "equal" number in each category. However, the number of females compared to males is increasing. In 1980, there were 110,053,161 males and 116,492,644 females. In 1984, of a total population of 236,681,000 there were 121,446,000 women and 115,236,000 men (Bureau of the Census 1984g, p. 24). Data until the year 2030 are given in table 6–1, indicating the growing number of women relative to men, which reflects the aging of our population and the fact that women outlive men.

Working Women, Mothers, and Wives

Statistics on the civilian labor force clearly show the striking changes that have occurred since the early 1970s. Whereas U.S. women had a labor force participation rate of 43.3 percent in 1970

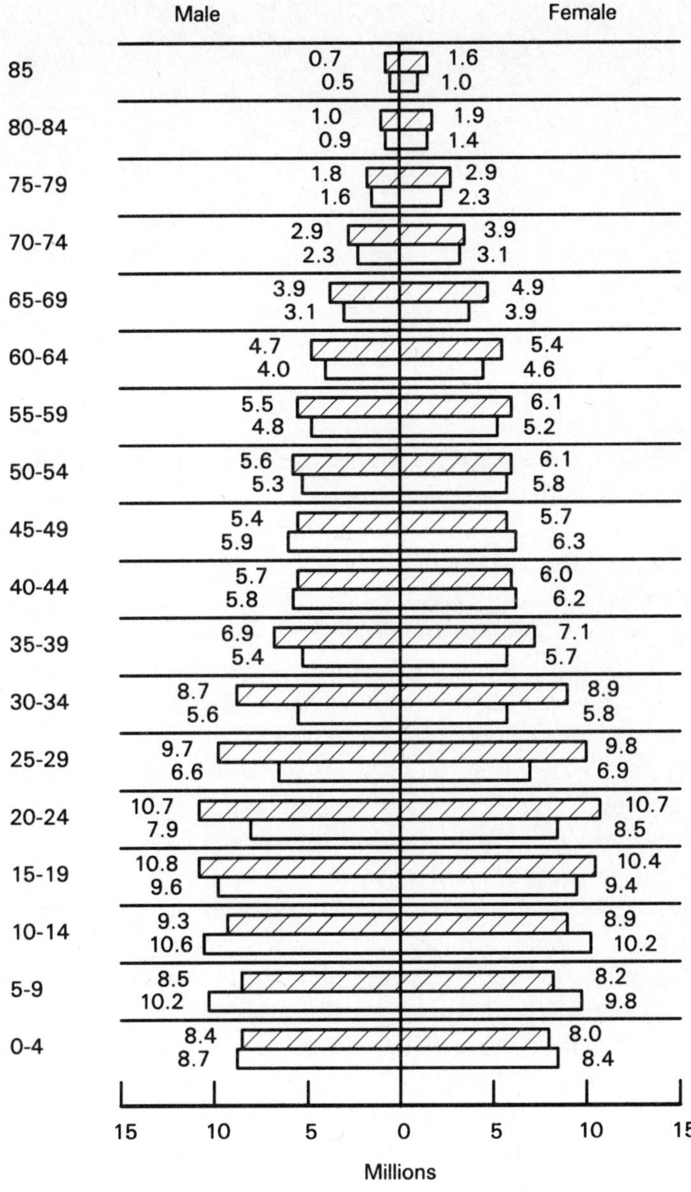

Source: Bureau of the Census 1980a, p. 1–12.

Figure 6–1. *Persons by Age and Sex: 1980 and 1970*

Table 6–1
Population Estimates by Sex: 1985–2030
(thousands)

	1985	*1990*	*1995*	*2000*	*2010*	*2020*	*2030*
Female	122,525	128,234	133,317	137,611	145,376	152,278	156,952
Male	116,123	121,497	126,314	130,379	137,765	144,061	147,378
Total	238,648	249,731	259,631	267,990	283,141	296,339	304,330
Female majority	6,402	6,737	7,003	7,232	7,611	8,217	9,574

Source: Bureau of the Census 1984d.

versus 79.7 percent for men, by 1985 that figure grew to 54.5 percent while the rate for men declined to 76.3 percent (Taeuber and Valdisera 1986, p. 3). Labor force participation rates are given in figure 6–2. About two-thirds of working-age women are in the labor force as are 60 percent of the women maintaining families (*Monthly Labor Review* 1983). The majority of new jobs created in the 1970s were taken up by women. But in times of economic difficulties they are far more likely than men to experience work interruptions (Bureau of the Census 1984b).

In just two-and-a-half decades, from the early 1960s to the present, the proportion of women keeping house full time versus the proportion in the labor force has flipflopped. As figure 6–3 shows, 50 percent kept house full time and 37 percent were in the labor force in 1962. By 1984, 53.5 percent were in the labor force; 33.4 percent were keeping house full time. It should be noted that only 41.8 percent, however, were in the labor force full time (Bianchi & Spain 1983; Statistical Abstract 1985, p. 398).

Families where both husband and wife are in the labor force now account for 52 percent of all married-couple families. And of the 32 million full-time homemakers in 1982, 60 percent were 45 years or older. Because labor-force participation seems to be related to age, given the aging of our population, and the growth of the middle-aged group, an even larger proportion of families with working wives in the future may well develop (Bianchi & Spain 1983).

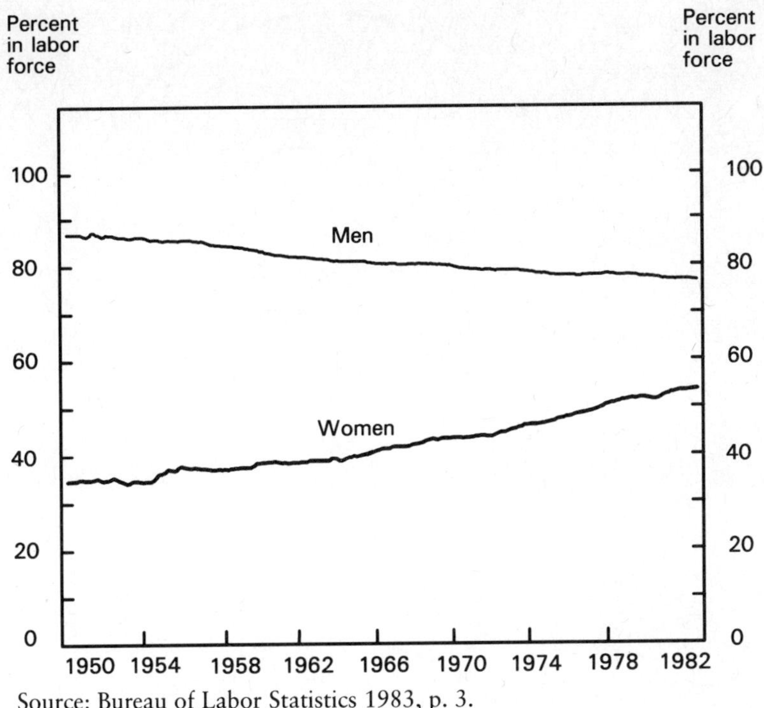

Source: Bureau of Labor Statistics 1983, p. 3.

Figure 6–2. *Women's Participation Rates*

The breakdown of the number and proportion of working women by marital status is shown in table 6–2. The bulk are married, over 28 million, or 59 percent; followed by those who were never married, over 12 million, 25.7 percent; and over 7 million widowed, divorced or separated, 15.4 percent.

It might reasonably be expected that a smaller proportion of wives would be in the labor force where husbands were present and where children were younger. Table 6–3 and figures 6–4 and 6–5 present relevant data. Table 6–3 shows the steady increase in the proportion of working wives from 23.8 percent in 1950 to 51.8 percent in 1983. Similarly, the proportion with children under 6 rose even more strikingly from 11.9 to 49.9 percent. The participation rate for wives with children 6 to 17 rose from 28.3 to 63.8 percent (Taeuber & Valdisera 1986). As figure 6–4 shows, compar-

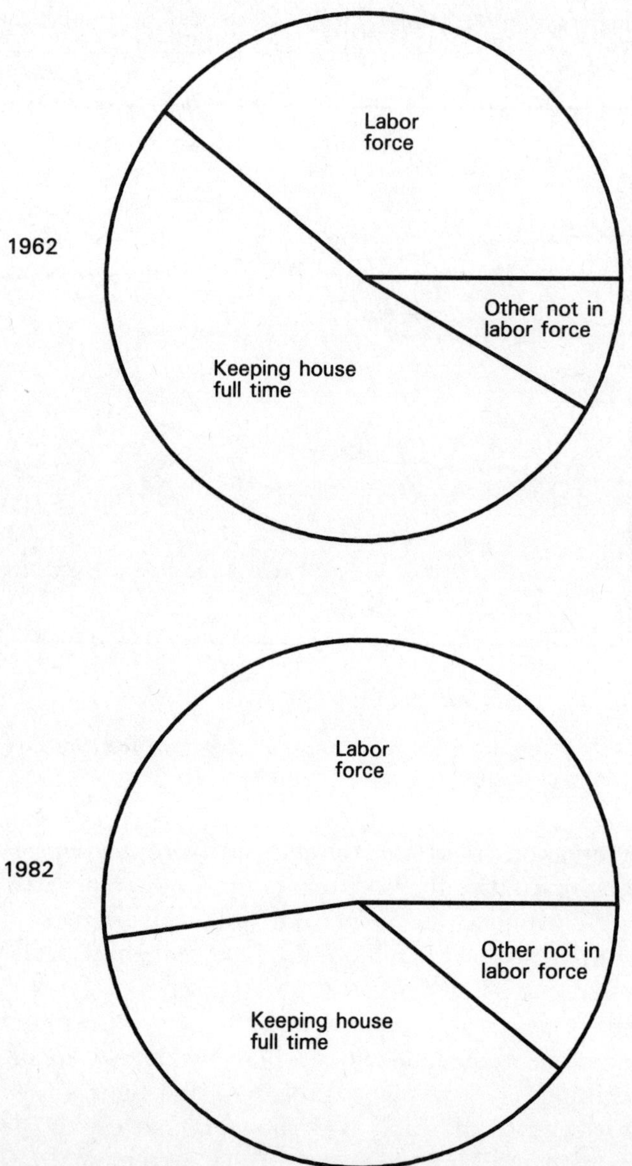

Source: Bureau of Labor Statistics 1983, p. 5.

Figure 6–3. *Labor Force Status of Women: 1962 and 1982*

Table 6–2
Women in the Labor Force: 1983

Marital Status	*In Labor Force (thousands)*	%
Married (husband present)	26,227	54.9
Married (husband absent)	1,913	4.0
Single (never married)	12,282	25.7
Widow, divorced, separated	7,357	15.4
Total	47,779	100.0

Source: *Monthly Labor Review* 1983.

Table 6–3
Labor Force Participation Rates of Married Women, Husband Present, by Presence and Age of Own Children: 1950–83

	Participation Rate				
			With Children under 18 Years		
Year	*Total*	*With No Children under 18 Years*	*Total*	*6–17 Years, None Younger*	*Under 6 Years*
1950	23.8	30.3	18.4	28.3	11.9
1960	30.5	34.7	27.6	39.0	18.6
1970	40.8	42.2	39.7	49.2	30.3
1971	40.8	42.1	39.7	49.4	29.6
1972	41.5	42.7	40.5	50.2	30.1
1973	42.2	42.8	41.7	50.1	32.7
1974	43.1	43.0	43.1	51.2	34.4
1975	44.4	43.8	44.9	52.2	36.7
1976	45.1	43.7	46.1	53.6	37.5
1977	46.6	44.8	48.2	55.5	39.4
1978	47.5	44.6	50.2	57.1	41.7
1979	49.3	46.6	51.9	59.0	43.3
1980	50.1	46.0	54.1	61.7	45.1
1981	51.0	46.3	55.7	62.5	47.8
1982	51.2	46.2	56.3	63.2	48.7
1983	51.8	46.6	57.2	63.8	49.9

Source: *Monthly Labor Review* 1983, p. 18.

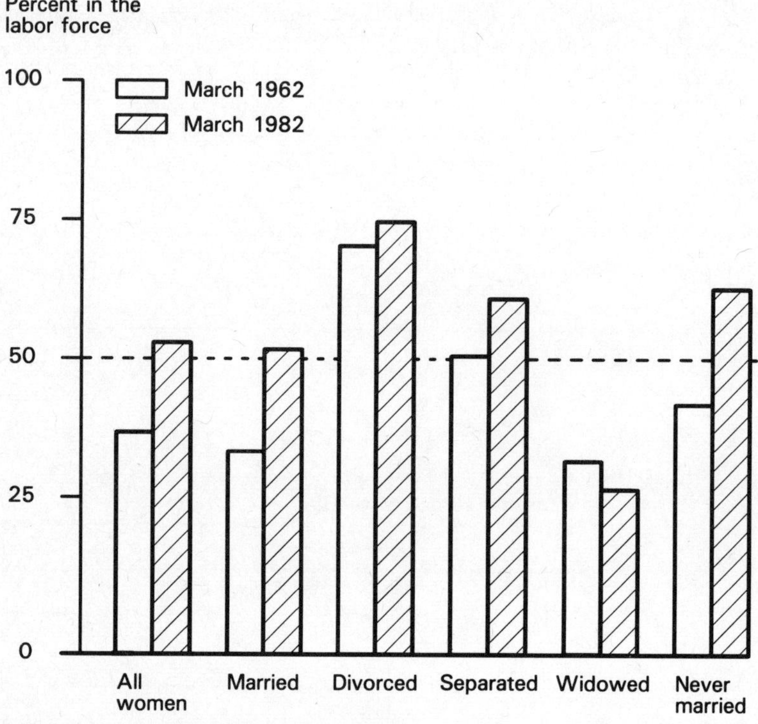

Source: Bureau of Labor Statistics 1983, p. 23.

Figure 6–4. *Labor-force Participation Rates by Marital Status: 1962 and 1982*

ing 1982 with 1962, of the 26 million wives in 1982 some 51 percent were in the labor force versus about one-third of all wives in 1962. A spurt occurred in the 1970s among wives with school-age children, regardless of age. There was also an increase in the participation of divorced, separated, and never-married women.

The data show the rapid growth in the proportion of working women and mothers over the past decade, and the decline in the proportion of working men. The presence of children does not result in nonworking mothers. In 1982, 55 percent of all children under 18—32 million—had a mother in the labor force. More than 45 percent of all children below 6 years of age, and almost 60 percent of those between 6 and 17, had working mothers (figure 6–5).

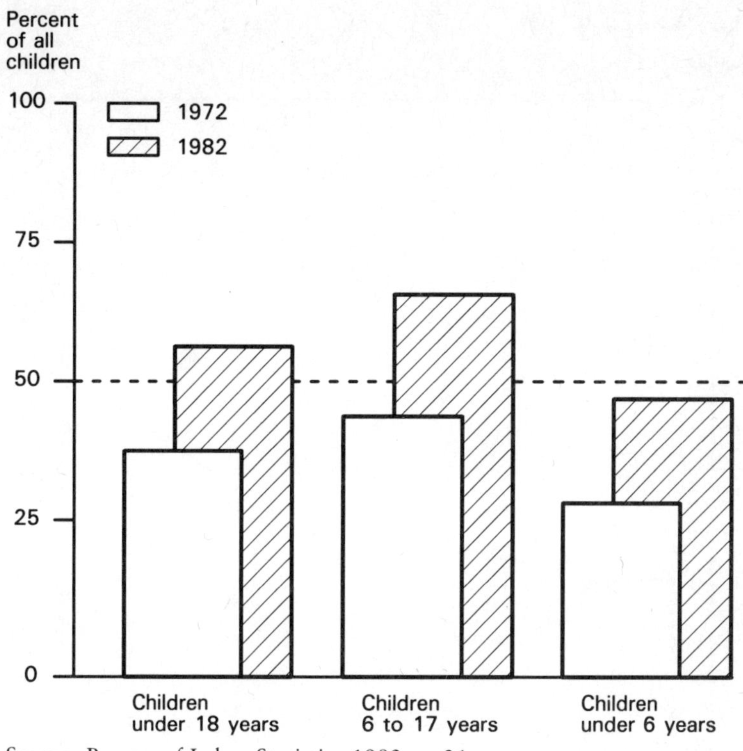

Source: Bureau of Labor Statistics 1983, p. 21.

Figure 6–5. *Children with Mothers in the Labor Force*

In 1983, half of the mothers with children under the age of 6 were in the labor force for the first time in history. It is expected that, very shortly, the majority of preschool children will have working mothers just as most school-age children do. This will amplify the demand for such child-care services as public and private nursery schools, family day-care centers, and all-day, part-day, and after-school care (Bianchi & Spain 1983).

The number and proportion of families maintained by women has increased steadily since 1960, as is shown in figure 6–6 and reached a new high in 1982—9.7 million—or about 1 of every 6 families. The growth rate of 57 percent far outstrips the 10 percent growth of total families, and reflects the increase in marital break-

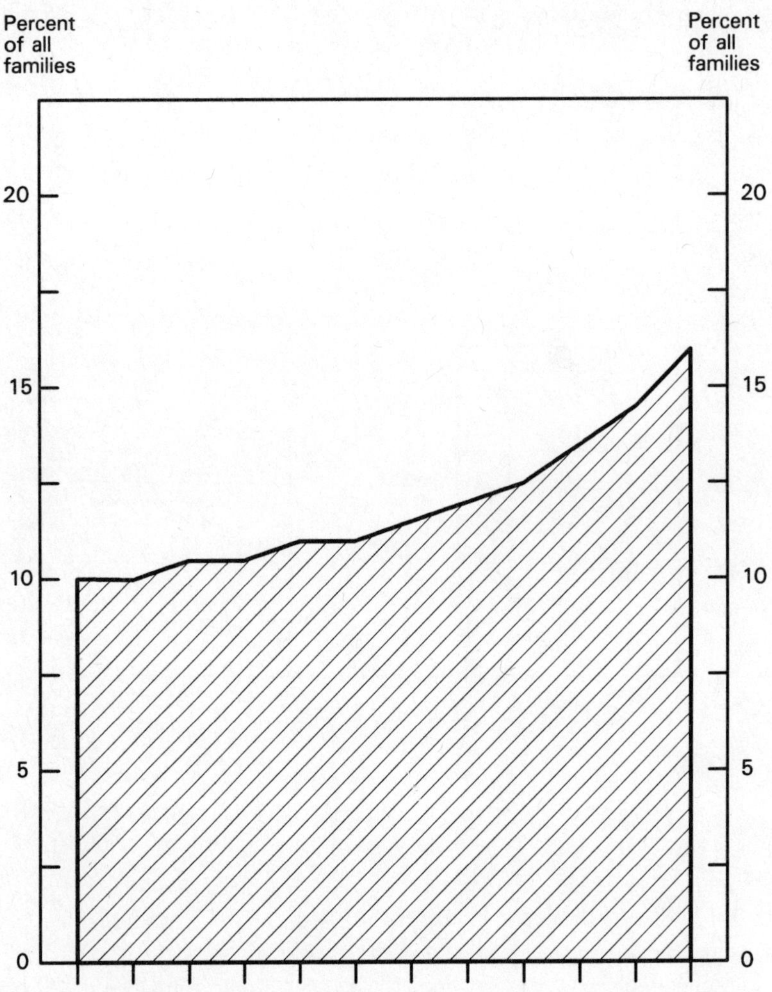

Source: Bureau of Labor Statistics 1983, p. 25.

Figure 6–6. *Families Maintained by Women as a Proportion of All Families: 1960–82*

ups and babies born out of wedlock. But families with breakups and out-of-wedlock babies are more likely to face economic difficulties. They are far more likely to have an unemployed head and live in poverty because they have an average income of less than half that of married families.

By way of summary, a review of figure 6–4 on women's labor force participation rates by marital status in 1962 and 1982 shows that growth occurred in the proportion of gainfully employed in all categories except for widows. Divorced women continue to have the highest labor-force participation rate, about 75 percent, followed by never-married and separated women. Women who are widows continue to have the lowest rate, probably because of their ages and wealth and income from estates. And these trends may well be accentuated in the near future.

Women's Occupations

The dramatic increase in women's labor-force participation rates probably has more far-reaching implications for our economy than any other change. Although women are found in every major industry group, and although the proportion of women in various positions is changing rapidly, they nevertheless remain concentrated in such traditionally female occupations as secretaries, nurses, school teachers, and retail selling. Women are especially concentrated in the services sector, and comprise almost 60 percent of all service employees. Most of the job gains realized by women have been in services, such as retailing, state, and local government. They accounted for 81 percent of all clerical workers, 97 percent of all private household services, and 60 percent of other services (Bianchi & Spain 1983).

Table 6–4 presents an occupational breakdown of working women in 1980. The highest concentration was in technical, sales, and administrative jobs, which comprised about 45 percent of women's jobs and where women were almost 65 percent of the labor force in that category. They are greatly underrepresented as a proportion of the labor force in precision production, craft, and repair (7.8 percent); farming, forestry, and fishing (14.9 percent); and operations, fabricators, and laborers (27.4 percent).

Table 6–4
Occupations of Working Women: 1980
(thousands)

Occupation	*Total*	*Females as a % of Total*
Managerial and professional	9,196	40.6
Technical, sales, and administrative	19,882	64.4
Service occupations	8,021	58.9
Farming, forestry, and fishing	451	14.9
Precision production, craft, and repair	1,056	7.8
Operators, fabricators, and laborers	5,486	27.4
Experienced unemployed	212	62.4
Total	44,304	42.6

Source: Bureau of the Census 1985, p. 400.

As in the past, working women only average about 60 percent of the earnings of their male counterparts. In 1980, white women averaged only 59 percent of white men's earnings; black women averaged 74 percent of black men's earnings (Bianchi & Spain 1983). Wives contribute significantly to a family's financial status and the proportion of family earnings they contribute has increased from 12 percent to 18 percent among whites (between 1972 and 1982) and from 17 percent to 28 percent among blacks.

Temporary or Full Time

A fairly common fallacy is that women only work temporarily or on a part-time basis. Yet, in 1984, 67.7 percent of adult women workers worked full-time, and 71.1 percent of them work 50 to 52 weeks per year. Though wives are less likely than their husbands to work full time year round, nevertheless 48.2 percent of all women workers did so (Bureau of the Census 1984g, p. 395).

Whether women work full time or not is associated with whether there are children under 18 at home. If so, the proportion of those working full time drops. Regardless, work life expectancy has increased sharply for women, as figure 6–7 shows, and an average 20-year-old can expect to spend more than 25 years in the labor force.

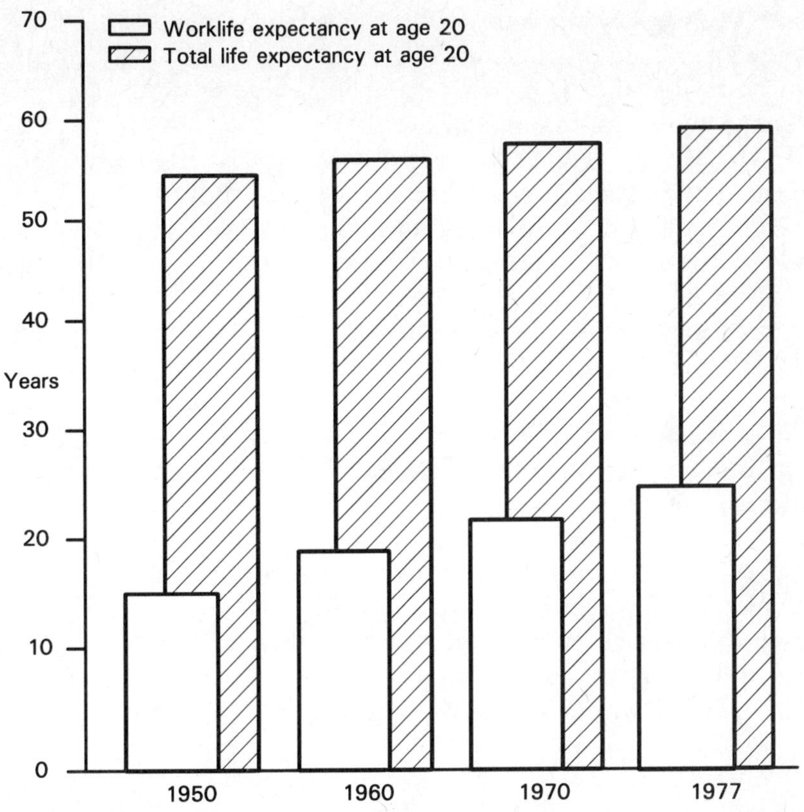

Source: Bureau of Labor Statistics 1983, p. 13.

Figure 6–7. *Worklife Expectancy of Women Age 20*

Why Do Women Work?

It is evident that economic necessity is the main stimulus for some working women, such as those who never married, are widowed, divorced, single parents, or who have unemployed husbands. For most married women, however, other reasons explain why over half are in the labor force. Most of them do, in fact, have husbands with good earnings so that strict economic necessity is not the major factor leading them to work. Yet, in about 25 percent of the families, women provide some 40 percent or more of family income.

A relationship clearly exists between fertility and labor-force participation. But it is not clear whether women limit their family size because they want to work or whether a smaller-sized family allows a woman the time to work. Even though they work, women still carry out the major part of the household tasks and have less time than men for leisure and sleep.

Historically, women have had lower levels of college enrollments and lower completion rates than men. But now the differences have been narrowed and the college enrollment and completion rates for women are similar to those for men. Though the gap is being closed in college degrees, the programs of study differ and women major more in education, humanities, and health services. As of 1983, 20 percent of men and 13 percent of women over 25 years of age have completed college. Eventually, there will be little difference between the sexes in completion rates.

The majority of working women, 45.5 percent, had four years of high school and about one-third had some college education, with 15 percent having four or more years of college. The higher the level of educational attainment, the greater the likelihood that women will be in the labor force, as is shown in table 6–5. Whereas only 18.3 percent of those who had less than 5 years of education are in the labor force, 57.1 percent with 4 years of high school and 72.5 percent with 5 or more years of college are employed. The

Table 6–5
Female Labor-force Participation by Education

Education	*% Who Work*
Elementary	
less than 5 years	18.3
5–7 years	23.8
8 years	24.5
High school	
1–3 years	42.2
4 years	57.1
College	
1–3 years	59.7
4 years	64.2
5 or more years	72.5

Source: Bianchi & Spain 1983.

labor-force participation rate for single women college graduates is 85 percent.

It is interesting that a larger proportion of wives with high-income husbands are in the labor force. A greater proportion of working wives occurs where husbands earn higher incomes than when they earn lower incomes, just the opposite of what one might expect. This may well reflect the educational levels of these wives, who are married to husbands with higher earning capabilities. The implications are that the income gap between working-wife and non–working-wife families will increase as will the number of wealthy working wives.

Married women often work so they can afford luxury and discretionary items; to extend their standard of living; to buy specific items such as a new home, a new car, or to travel; to meet rising expectations; to escape from the home and gain independence; to broaden their horizons and receive social stimulation; and of course, to realize themselves by practicing their professions. Throughout history, wealthy women sought to escape from the toil and drudgery of bringing up a family and doing household chores. Now, for the first time and to a greater extent, so can women from middle- and lower-class homes. Technology is now available to reduce some of the labor necessary to keep a house running, freeing middle- and lower-income women from some of the time-consuming household tasks.

Working women, particularly working wives, have encouraged a substantial shift in thinking about women's careers and family responsibilities in a relatively short time span. Wives no longer need to sublimate their personal needs and professional and career aspirations. As a result, they have become more independent, which is partly reflected in our rising number of divorces. And men now share in family adjustments and think about combining their own careers with those of their wives.

There is an increasing propensity for women to become more independent and to form and manage their own households. Substantial increases in the proportion doing so occurred for every age group. In 1980, over one-half of all women 65 and over, as well as young single women, were maintaining their own independent residences. This is directly related to the increased labor-force participation resulting in economic ability to do so.

The dividing lines between mens' and womens' work on the job and at home has blurred. Increasing educational opportunities for women have opened up new kinds of career opportunities and women are moving into previously male-dominated professions and trades. In a similar manner, men are also moving into some of the traditional female careers such as flight attendant, nursing, and secretarial jobs. No longer does social convention constrain women and men as tightly.

With such a large proportion of working mothers, teenagers and fathers now perform some of the family shopping, cooking, and other household chores. Products that reduce both the drudgery and time spent on household chores by automating household activities are in increasing demand. Between one-half and one-third of all meals are now cooked outside the home. Convenience is the byword, with fully prepared foods, whether fresh, frozen, or catered, exhibiting remarkable growth. And women who might have felt guilty about feeding their families at fast-food restaurants in the past now justify their situations by the fact that they are "bringing home the bacon" and simply do not have the time to function in some of the traditional household roles.

How, in the 1950s and 1960s could wives have justified purchasing a $400 to $500 microwave oven just to heat food? Nor could they have felt comfortable about taking their families to restaurants instead of cooking or having family members handle individual feeding and household support activities and going their own way. In our new society, however, with the large increase in working women, these approaches are commonplace. This presages the performance of more household tasks and activities outside the home and suggests the need for new services provided at convenient times and places for the members of the female labor force.

As a large proportion of women enter the labor force, charitable and community organizations continue to lose tremendous assets, the physical and mental capacities of volunteer women. How will they ever replace them? They are not able to afford purchasing similar services on the market. What will happen to our charities? Will the elderly, who are healthier than in the past and who are retiring earlier, and living longer, pick up the slack?

Many questions concerning the future economic and social impact of working women remain unanswered. What will the effect be on latch-key children (those who come home to an empty house)? Will they be better or worse off as a result? Will working women increasingly suffer from the same stress illnesses such as ulcers and hypertension that men do? Are women who pursue careers more satisfied than those who stay home and dedicate themselves to family upbringing? With more working wives, is the poverty of time now becoming a more important constraint on family purchases and consumption? These are illustrative of the significant life-style questions that cannot be answered with our statistical data.

Summary

The growing proportion of working women, particularly wives and mothers, has been the most dramatic socioeconomic change of the past 20 years. Our mores have changed so that working women, particularly married women, are now accepted as a normal part of the U.S. life-style. The population triangle indicates that the overall shape of the age distribution of both sexes is similar, although females outnumbered males in 1984 by over 6 million.

In 1983, women comprised 43 percent of the labor force. The majority of new jobs created in the 1970s were taken up by women. The proportion of women in the labor force rose to 53.5 percent in 1984; the proportion who kept house full time dropped to 33.4 percent. Fifty-two percent of all married-couple families have both husband and wife in the labor force and this proportion is projected to increase. By 2000 over two-thirds of all wives may be gainfully employed.

The proportion of working wives with children under 6, and with children under 18, has risen dramatically. A spurt occurred in the 1970s among all wives with school-aged children regardless of age. In 1982, 55 percent of all children under 18—32 million—had a mother in the labor force. The year 1983 marked the first time that half of the mothers with children under 6 were in the labor force.

Both the number and proportion of families headed by women have increased steadily since 1980 reaching 9.7 million in 1982.

There has been an increase in family breakups and children born out of wedlock, both situations associated with higher rates of unemployment and poverty. Divorced women have the highest labor-force participation rate, 75 percent, followed by never-married and separated women. Widows continue to have the lowest rate.

Though the proportion of women in various occupations is changing, there are concentrations in such traditional female occupations as secretaries, nurses, school teachers, and retail selling. Women comprised about 60 percent of all service employees in 1982 and accounted for 81 percent of all clerical workers and 97 percent of all household services. Technical, sales, and administrative jobs make up about 45 percent of women's jobs. Women are greatly under represented in precision production, craft, and repair.

Women workers average only 60 percent of the earnings of their male counterparts. The proportion of family earnings contributed by women in 1982 rose to 18 percent among whites and to 28 percent among blacks. In about 25 percent of the families women provide some 40 percent or more of family income. Women workers are full-time workers for the most part—67.7 percent of adult women workers worked full time in 1984. Wives are less likely than husbands to work full time and this seems to be related to children under 18 being at home. Regardless, work expectancy for women has increased sharply.

Economic necessity is the main reason that many women work. But for most married women there are other reasons such as to practice their profession, to purchase discretionary items, or to contribute to a better family life-style. There is a higher proportion of working wives among families where husbands have higher incomes. Although women historically have had lower college completion rates than men, they are now similar. A much higher proportion of college-educated women is in the labor force as compared with noncollege educated women.

A substantial shift in thinking about women's careers and family responsibilities has occurred and women no longer need sublimate their personal and professional needs. There is an increasing propensity for women to become more independent and form their own households. New career opportunities have opened up and social convention no longer constrains them as tightly. Many interesting questions about the future economic and social impact of working women remain unanswered.

References

Bianchi, Suzanne M., and Daphne Spain. 1983. "American Women: Three Decades of Change." Bureau of the Census. CDS 80-8.

Bureau of the Census. 1970. *1970 Census of Population: Volume II Reports:* "Persons of Spanish Origin."

———. 1980a. *Census of Population: Volume I Reports.* Chapter B, U.S. Summary, Series no. PC89-1-B1.

———. 1980b. *A Portrait of Women in the United States.* Series P-23, no. 100 (February).

———. 1982a. *Fertility of American Women: June 1980.* Series P-20, no. 375 (October).

———. 1982b. *Household and Family Characteristics: March 1982.*

———. 1982c. *Marital Status and Living Arrangements: March 1982.*

———. 1982d. *Money Income of Households, Families, and Persons in the United States: 1981.*

———. 1982e. *Persons of Spanish Origin in the United States: March 1982.* Series P-20, no. 396.

———. 1983a. *After-Tax Money Income Estimates of Households: 1983.*

———. 1983b. *Household Families, Marital Status, and Living Arrangements: March 1983.* Series P-20, no. 382 (July).

———. 1984a. *Childspacing among Birth Cohorts of American Women: 1905 to 1959.* Series P-20, no. 385 (April).

———. 1984b. *Detailed Occupation of the Experienced Civilian Labor Force by Sex for the United States and Regions: 1980 and 1970.*

———. 1984c. *Homeownership Trends: 1983.* Series H-121 (May).

———. 1984d. *Lifetime Work Experience and Its Effect on Earnings.* Series P-23, no. 136.

———. 1984e. *Marital Status and Living Arrangements: March 1983.* Series P-20, no. 389 (July).

———. 1984f. *Projections of the Population of the United States by Age, Sex, and Race: 1983 to 2080.* Series P-25, no. 952.

———. 1984g. *Statistical Abstract of the United States: 1985.*

Bureau of Labor Statistics. 1983. *Women at Work: A Chartbook* (April).

Department of Housing and Urban Development. 1985. *General Housing Characteristics: 1983 Annual Housing Survey.* Series H-150-83A.

Kelley, Jack. 1985. "One-Parent Homes Soar to 1 in 4." *USA TODAY* (15 May):1.

Matney, William C., and Dwight L. Johnson. 1983. *America's Black Population: 1970 to 1982*. Washington, D.C.: Bureau of the Census.

Monthly Labor Review. 1983. "Family Labor Force Statistics" (December).

———. 1984. "Occupational Reclassification and Changes in Distribution by Gender" (March).

Taeuber, Cynthia M., and Victor Valdisera. 1986. "Women in the American Economy." Bureau of the Census. Series P-23, no. 146 (November).

7
Living Arrangements: Households and Families

Introduction

Households are determinants, not only of the demand for consumer products, but for such industrial products as steel, cement, and lumber. The demand for housing is one of the closely watched indicators of the general well-being of our economy. As the vice president of a furniture and home furnishings chain remarked, "We keep our eyes glued on data about households: as they go, so goes our business."

In this chapter, we shall consider the variety of households and living arrangements, and their trends and tendencies. Included will be discussions of home ownership, singles' households, unmarried-couples households, family and married households. Attention is given to the impact of trends in household size, marriage, and divorce.

Home Ownership

Our living arrangements have changed greatly since the mid-1960s, culminating in changing market opportunities. The dynamic shifts in the number and types of households are reflected by changes in families, marriages, divorce, and singleness. The impact is felt on the demand for houses, apartments, appliances, furniture, furnishings, food, and a host of complementary products and services. There is a strong home ownership ethic in the United States, and owning one's home is part of the "American Dream." It is bolstered

Table 7–1
Home Ownership Rates

Year	*Rate (%)*
1940	43.6
1950	55.0
1960	61.9
1970	62.9
1980	65.6
1983	64.6

Source: Bureau of the Census, 1984b.
Note: Home ownership rate is the percentage of households that own their own homes.

by tax considerations. The growth of home ownership has been an important part of our economic scene.

In 1985, there were 86.8 million households in the United States, and they featured more amenities than was the case a decade earlier. Included among the amenities are extra bathrooms, complete kitchens, warm-air furnaces, heat pumps, steam and hot-water systems, and the like. Between 1973 and 1983, married couples increased their share of occupied housing units from 74 to 77 percent and the proportion who rent fell from 26 to 23 percent (Department of Housing and Urban Development 1985).

Estimates are that the United States' 100 millionth housing unit will be completed in March 1987. The 89.7 million occupied housing units in 1986 consisted of: 1 unit, 67.1 percent; 2–4 units, 12.4 percent; 5 or more units, 16.2 percent; mobile homes, 4.4 percent. Of these, 57.3 million were owner-occupied and 32.4 million were renter-occupied (Census 1987).

But in 1983, for the first time since the census started keeping records of quarterly home ownership rates in 1962, there was a drop in the percentage of householders owning their own homes. Home ownership rates are given in table 7–1. Perhaps this merely reflects temporary recent economic difficulties and high interest rates.

Table 7–2
Growth in Households: 1965–2000
(millions)

Year	*Number of Households*
1965	57.3
1970	63.4
1975	71.1
1980	80.8
1985	86.8
1990	92.0
1995	98.5
2000	104.5

Source: Bureau of the Census 1985, and author's projections (for 1990–2000).

Household Growth

Households, both family (a related group of 2 or more persons living in a household) and nonfamily (households headed by a male or a female or two persons not related) are primary buying units. Table 7–2 presents data, actual and projected totals, on household growth from 1965 to 2000.

The growth of households varies with such economic factors as interest rates, as well as marriages, divorces, and age structures. It slowed from an annual rate of 1.6 million during the 1970s to about 1 million in the early 1980s. In 1985, it increased to about 1.9 million. Estimates are that we shall need a minimum of over 2 million net new households each year for the next 20 years just to maintain, not improve, the quality of our housing. The question is how can we get them, for we did not even approach that figure in the recent past.

Housing in the United States has passed the point of being considered a privilege and has taken on the position of a right. Consumers feel that they have a right to adequate housing.

Some families have two or more homes, including the vacation farm or home and the regular family home. But unlike the situation in many other countries, the family home is quite temporary. It is the vacation home, or the family farm, that seems to stay in the family for generations as families move in and out of their regular housing. U.S. families change addresses about once every six years as their housing needs change. Many first try to obtain a foothold in the housing market by purchasing a small house, condominium, or apartment, which gives them both tax benefits and the opportunity to trade up to a more desirable house later. Surprisingly, single individuals have often bought houses much larger than they need, as investments, tax shelters, and hedges against inflation.

Household Types

Basically, there are two types of households: family and nonfamily. Family households consist of three types: married-couple, and others with either a male householder or female householder, as is shown in table 7–3. Family households made up 81.2 percent of all households in 1970, declined sharply to 73.7 percent in 1980 and to 73.2 percent in 1983. Conversely, in the 10-year period 1970–80, nonfamily households grew about 50 percent from 18.8 to 26.3 percent. Although family households increased by about 10 million over the 1970–83 period, nonfamily households almost doubled, adding approximately 11 million households (Bureau of the Census 1984b).

Table 7–3
Households, by Type: 1983, 1980, and 1970
(thousands)

	1983		*1980*		*1970*	
Type of Household	*Number*	*%*	*Number*	*%*	*Number*	*%*
Total households	83,918	100.0	80,776	100.0	63,401	100.0
Family households	61,393	73.2	59,550	73.7	51,456	81.2
Married-couple family	49,908	59.5	49,112	60.8	44,728	70.5
Other family, male householder	2,015	2.4	1,733	2.1	1,228	1.9
Other family, female householder	9,470	11.3	8,705	10.8	5,500	8.7
Nonfamily households	22,525	26.8	21,226	26.3	11,945	18.8
Male householder	9,514	11.3	8,801	10.9	4,063	6.4
Female householder	13,011	15.5	12,419	15.4	7,882	12.4
Living alone	19,250	22.9	18,296	22.7	10,851	17.1

Source: Bureau of the Census, 1984c, p. 6.

Married-couple households, the most common perception of a household, traditionally have accounted for about three-fourths of all households. From 1970 to 1983 they increased absolutely from 44 to 49 million, but fell proportionately from 70.5 to 59.5 percent, as is shown in table 7–3. They are projected to fall further, perhaps to 52 percent, by 1995.

Family households with a male householder (no wife) increased from 1.2 million to 2 million between 1970 and 1983 and those with a female householder (no husband) grew from 5.5 to 9.5 million. These single-parent families headed by a female grew by some 72 percent, and while total family households increased by 10 million, those maintained by women accounted for an amazing 40 percent of that growth.

Census Bureau estimates indicate that over one in four U.S. families with children (26 percent) has only one parent living at home. This is an increase for single-family parents from 22 percent in 1980, and 13 percent in 1970. The majority of children, an estimated 60 percent, will live with a single parent before age 18. Of black family groups with children, 59 percent have one parent, an increase from 35.7 percent in 1970 (Kelley 1985). Single-parent households have become a major market segment; factors supporting the trend are separations, divorces, and births out of wedlock. The demand for child-care services will increase and such services could become widely sought employee benefits. Estimates are that by 1990 working mothers will need care for 10.4 million children.

Size of Households

The dramatic increase of singles' households coupled with the trend to smaller-sized families have supported an uninterrupted decline in average household size for the last quarter century. In 1960, the size was 3.33 persons; by 1983 it fell to 2.73. Such changes reverberate throughout a wide variety of public- and private-sector industries affecting the demand for everything from houses, cars, food, and clothing to aid to dependent children, the military, and schools.

Table 7–4 deals with household size from 1960 to 1984. It underscores the rapid increase in one-person households, some increase in two-person households, and a proportionate decrease in all the rest. The most striking decreases are in the 5-, 6-, and 7-

Table 7–4
Household Size: 1960–84
(as % of total)

	1960	*1970*	*1980*	*1982*	*1984*
Total (millions)	52.6	63.4	80.8	83.5	85.4
% of total					
1 person	13.1	17.1	22.7	23.2	23.4
2 persons	27.8	28.9	31.4	31.7	31.5
3 persons	18.9	17.3	17.5	17.5	17.7
4 persons	17.6	15.8	15.7	15.4	15.9
5 persons	11.5	10.3	7.5	7.3	7.1
6 persons	5.7	5.6	3.1	3.0	2.8
7 persons	5.4	5.0	2.2	1.9	1.6

Source: Bureau of the Census 1983b, 1985.

person households, which by 1920 and 1930 standards were not considered large, for in 1920 the average household size was about 4.3 persons per household. Now such households are considered a rarity.

An interesting scenario develops when the trends of decreasing household size and rising household incomes are considered. The result is that per-capita incomes increase significantly, particularly among married-couple families. Consumers have more income to spend on themselves. Smaller-sized families also mean that parents may have more time to spend on each child, should they so choose. This could present an unprecedented opportunity of developing more knowledgeable, better adjusted and informed children—it is a chance to increase the effectiveness of parenting when both parents are present.

Singles

Although most people live in families, and historically 96 percent of the U.S. population married, the very rapid doubling of nonfamily households in itself is a striking phenomenon. In 1984, there were an amazing 19.9 million single-person households, almost double the 10.8 million households in 1970 (Bureau of the Census

1985, p. 40). About four times as many 25–34-year-olds maintained their own households in 1984 as in 1970. (Bureau of the Census 1984, p. 1). As important for marketers is the fact that most of them are made up of people living alone.

An increasing proportion of Americans over 30 are single. Singleness results from divorce and separation, as well as the postponement of marriage. Both males and females of marriage age have delayed marriage by almost two-and-one-half years. About two-thirds of singles' households are occupied by women, although the number of single male households is increasing rapidly, having doubled in the 1970s.

For most young and divorced people, however, living alone is usually just a transitional stage before marriage. Yet, it is expected that a larger number and proportion of our citizens will remain single.

Against this backdrop one can well understand such developments as the single-serving packages, smaller sized appliances, sports cars, smaller containers, the construction of singles' apartments, the sale of frozen and freshly prepared foods, the increasing number of delicatessens in supermarkets, and the increase in meals eaten outside the home.

Unmarried Couples

Changes in our mores (coupled with such factors as later age of marriage, higher divorce rates, more women in the work force, and even the quirks of our tax laws that grant unmarried couples lower tax rates than married couples) have resulted in a wider variety of acceptable living arrangements than was previously the case. The number of unmarried-couple households has had a striking increase, more than tripling between 1970 and 1983, but that trend has slowed since 1983. Though they reached a high of 1.9 million households, that still is just 4 percent of all married-couple households and certainly does not herald the demise of marriages. Rather, many of the unmarried couples wind up marrying. Most of these couples, 72 percent, do not have any children under 15, and for the most part, they are now younger than their 1970 counterparts. In 1983, 8 of 10 of these households were maintained by someone under age 45 versus only 3 of ten in 1970 (Bureau of the Census 1984c).

Not a great deal is known about the purchase reactions of unmarried households. The potential instability of the relationship adds an interesting dimension. As the female partner of an unmarried couple explained, "You might not want to go out and buy a washer and dryer, but you would sure expect to have the convenient use of one." Perhaps they present a market for rentals, leases with options to buy, and for shorter-lasting and less expensive durable goods.

Marriages

Notwithstanding all the criticisms and the oft-made predictions of the demise of marriage, the ballooning number of divorces, and the 1960s theme that "communes will replace the outmoded institution of marriage," marriages have been thriving. (Some of them are remarriages). They have been growing steadily and persistently since 1960 (table 7–5). When couples marry, markets for a wide variety of products are affected, not merely those associated with weddings,

Table 7–5
Marriages 1960–1983
(thousands)

Year	*Total*
1960	1,523
1965	1,800
1970	2,159
1975	2,153
1980	2,390
1981	2,438
1982	2,495
1983	2,444[a]
1984	2,487[a]

Source: Bureau of the Census 1985.
[a]Preliminary figures.

but those of such diverse areas as housing, cement, steel, lumber, food, autos, clothing, furniture, appliances, and home furnishings.

Since 1960, with the exception of 1983, the number of marriages has increased steadily, reaching 2.44 million in 1983. This is a function of the baby bust during the Great Depression of the 1930s and the baby boom after World War II. There were over 50 percent more marriages in 1980 than there were in 1960. Although 1983 marked a slight decline of 2 percent in marriages, they were still 60 percent higher than in 1960.

Both men and women are marrying later in life. The median age of first marriage has increased about 2.5 years since 1960. For males it rose from 22.8 years in 1960 to 25.4 years in 1983, and for females it increased from 20.3 to 22.8 years (table 7–6).

The average age of first marriage for men is about 2.5 years higher than it is for women, but females' life expectancy is approximately 8 years longer than it is for men. It is evident that in the future the proportion of widows will grow. And men in their later years could become a widely sought, scarce resource. The marriage age trend from the turn of the century to the mid-1950s was to get married earlier. Since then, however, the tendency has been reversed and the 1983 data are similar to those of 1890. The young are just postponing marriage, not forgoing it, and are extending the time spent on their working careers. Historically, 96 percent of men and

Table 7–6
Median Age of First Marriage

	Men	*Women*
1890	26.1	22.0
1910	25.1	21.6
1940	24.3	21.5
1955	22.6	20.2
1960	22.8	20.3
1970	23.2	20.8
1980	24.7	22.0
1983	25.4	22.8

Source: Bureau of the Census 1984c, p. 1.

Table 7–7
Marital Status of the Population 18 and Over
(numbers in millions and % of total number)

	1960		*1970*		*1980*		*1982*	
	Number	*%*	*Number*	*%*	*Number*	*%*	*Number*	*%*
Single (never married)	27.7	22.0	21.4	16.2	32.3	20.3	34.4	20
Married	84.4	67.3	95.0	71.7	104.6	65.5	106.2	64
Widowed	10.6	8.4	11.8	8.3	12.7	8.0	12.7	7
Divorced	2.9	2.3	4.3	3.2	9.9	6.2	11.5	7
Total	125.5		132.5		159.5		164.7	

Source: Bureau of the Census 1983a.

women have married at some time in their life. Regardless of divorces, married persons typically remain married; most have children, and most husbands and wives have similar education levels—quite the conventional scene.

The marital status of our population 18 and over is shown in table 7–7. The table indicates the actual number in millions and the percent of that total. Though the actual numbers in each category have increased, the proportions reveal some of the dynamics at work. As might be expected, the proportion of population that is divorced has tripled from 1960 to 1982. Singles (in the sense of never having been married) have increased from 16.2 percent in 1970 to 20.9 percent in 1982. The proportion of married and widowed people has decreased.

The proportion of young adults who have never married has increased dramatically. For women aged 30–34, in 1983, that proportion was more than twice as high as in 1970. The rate also increased significantly for "older" women between 1970 and 1983, from 19 percent to 38 percent for 25–29-year-olds, and from 9 to 20 percent for the 30–34-year-olds. Among young men aged 20–24, the percentage of unmarried has risen about one-third, from 55 percent in 1970 to 73 percent in 1983. An unanswered question is whether this merely represents postponement of marriage or whether it indicates a trend to unmarried persons (Bureau of the

Census 1984c, p. 1–4). In 1983, only 4 percent of U.S. men and women had never married by the time they reached the 55–64-year-old age group. In the future, though the bulk of people will undoubtedly marry, it seems that there will be a higher proportion remaining single throughout their lives—perhaps 15 percent of all women. The chances of marrying decrease very rapidly for women over age 30.

Families

We are a family-oriented country, and families are a basic unit of our society—they represent some of the strongest human bonds. They mold the character of the work force, pass on values and standards, and shape purchasing behavior and consumption patterns. Yet neither business nor government policies seem to reflect this orientation and the family changes that have occurred. Nevertheless, our family ties are seen in widely quoted, but not necessarily correct sayings: "Like mother like daughter" and "like father like son."

Since the turbulent 1960s, the family as an institution, like marriage, has been under attack. It too was thought by some to be an outmoded institution. The 1970s were years of great stress on families as a result of high unemployment, inflation, changing life-styles and mores, the employment of wives, and the increasing divorce rate. There have been lots of changes among families, particularly in composition, as well as changes that are not so obvious. Regardless, families in general continue to thrive and are doing well.

The widely accepted notion is that the typical U.S. family consists of a mother, father with 2 children (preferably a boy and a girl), with the father as the breadwinner and the mother at home. However, that is grossly misleading, for families of this kind represent only about 1 in 16 of all U.S. families.

Families have certainly been in a state of flux and transition since the mid-1960s, and have changed dramatically from an extended structure to a nuclear one. They have become much smaller and, as we noted, more of today's school-age and preschool children than ever before are living with one parent, or stepparent. These children have a higher proportion of working mothers than ever.

The phenomenon of latch-key children, children who come home from school to an empty house, is on the rise. The impact of the trend on the children, and on our economy and society, is not yet clear.

Despite such changes, married-couple families still predominate. They accounted for 80 percent of all families in 1980, and now comprise about 8 of 10 white families, 7 of 10 Hispanic families, and 5 of 10 black families.

Table 7–8 presents data on family types from 1940 to 1983. In this 43-year period the total number of married couples has almost doubled. The families maintained by women, however, have almost tripled, and an additional 500,000 men are maintaining their own families. More than half of all married couples have become multiearner families and the proportion of the labor force that is female,

Table 7–8
Families by Type, Selected Years: 1940–83
(thousands)

			Other Families		
				Maintained by Women	
Year	*All Families*	*Married-couple Families*	*Maintained by Men*	*Total*	*As % of All Families*
1940	32,166	26,971	1,579	3,616	11.2
1947	35,794	31,211	1,186	3,397	9.5
1950	39,303	34,440	1,184	3.679	9.4
1955	41,951	36,378	1,339	4,234	10.1
1960	45,062	39,293	1,275	4,494	10.0
1965	47,836	41,649	1,181	5,006	10.5
1970	51,227	44,415	1,239	5,580	10.9
1975	56,257	47,528	1,412	7,316	13.0
1980	59,910	49,132	1,769	9,009	15.0
1983	61,834	49,947	2,059	9,828	15.9

Source: Waldman 1983, p. 17.

Note: Data were collected in April of 1940, 1947, and 1955, and in March of all other years. Data for 1975 have been revised since initial publication.

as we have already noted, has risen to about 45 percent (*Monthly Labor Review* 1983).

The other side of the coin of the increase in children living with a single parent is the significant decline in both the number and proportion of children living with both parents. It has dropped from 58.9 million in 1970 to 46.8 million in 1982. This is a 21-percent decrease and in 1982 only 75 percent of them lived with both parents compared with 85 percent in 1970. This occurred in light of a 10-percent decline in the actual number of children under 18 over the period.

In addition to an increasing number of young adults establishing their own households, there has also been a striking change in the number of them who still live at home with their parents. Of all young adults, those aged 18–24 have the largest proportion at home—54 percent. Between 1970 and 1983 there was a 117-percent increase in the 25–34 age group living at home. The reasons for this include high unemployment, high divorce rates, and slower economic growth (which affects starting salaries).

At the other end of the spectrum are the changes in the living arrangements of elderly families. (We shall investigate mature consumers in chapter 8.) Great shifts have occurred in the living patterns of the noninstitutionalized 75-and-over group (the older olders), more so than for the 65–74-year-olds (the middle olders). The proportion of people 75 years old and older living with relatives in families declined from 64 percent in 1970 to 59 percent in 1983. And 7 out of 10 of the 5.8 million persons 75 and over in families were husbands and wives still maintaining their own families, with 40 percent of them maintaining their own households.

For those 65–74 years old, the 1970–83 data showed no changes. In 1983, 72 percent were living with relatives and 62 percent of them were living as husbands and wives (Bureau of the Census 1984c).

Divorce

Although 96 percent of our population historically have married at some point in their lives, an increasing number of them have had their marriages dissolved by divorce. The acceptance of divorce by our society, a phenomenon of the 1960s and 1970s, reflects a change in our mores. But, an increase in the number of divorces should not be interpreted as disenchantment or rebellion against marriage. Rather, it reflects dissatisfaction with a particular partner. In any event an increase in divorce results in a larger number of families being maintained by women.

The median duration of a marriage since 1960 has been about 7 years. Most divorced people tend to remarry, but the ratio is higher for men than women, resulting in a higher divorce ratio for women (divorced persons per 1,000 married persons living with their spouses)—80 percent of divorced men and 75 percent of divorced women do remarry. An estimated 45 percent of all new marriages are second marriages. In 1983, the divorce rate was 137/1,000 women versus 91/1,000 men. An estimated 45 percent of second marriages also end in divorce.

Since the mid-1960s, the likelihood of divorce has reached record levels, while that of marriage has declined. The divorce rate rose to 114 divorced persons per 1,000 married people in 1982 versus 47 in 1970. The actual number of divorces in 1983 reached 1,179,000, 50 percent of the number of marriages. The chances of a marriage ending in divorce are now estimated to be about 1 in 2. In 1983, of those aged 25–29, which has generally been a high marriage group, one-fourth of the women and one-third of the men had yet to marry (Bureau of the Census 1985).

Table 7–9 summarizes selected divorce statistics for the period 1960–83. Prior to this, in 1940, there was but 1 divorce for every 6 marriages; in 1982 the figure shot up to a striking 1 divorce for every 2 marriages.

As table 7–9 indicates, both the number of divorces and the divorce rate (the number of divorces granted per 1,000 population) slowed down in the 1980s. For the second successive year, a slight decrease was seen in 1983, and the preliminary estimates for 1984 are a further decline to 4.9 (Bureau of the Census 1985, p. 56). The question remains whether this is the start of a trend or just a little squiggle in an upward persistent thrust. Regardless, estimates are that 1 in 2 marriages will result in divorce.

The median age of divorce after the first marriage has been in-

Table 7–9
Divorces: 1960–83

Year	*Number of Marriages (thousands)*	*Number of Divorces (thousands)*	*Divorce Rate*	*Divorce Ratio*
1960	1,523	393	2.2	35
1970	2,159	708	3.5	47
1980	2,390	1,189	5.2	100
1982	2,495	1,180	5.1	114
1983	2,440	1,179	5.0	—

Source: Bureau of the Census 1985.

creasing steadily from 1965 to 1982. For males it has increased from 30.5 to 33.6 years and for females from 27.9 to 31.1 years. The higher the education and the higher the level of job responsibility, the greater the chance of divorce. Persons 30–44 years old have the highest divorce ratio of any age group. Although the divorce ratio has increased in all age categories since 1960, the biggest proportionate increase has been in the under-30 category, followed by the 30–44 age category. As increasing numbers of our population enter this age bracket, over the next 15 years our divorce rates might increase. If they do, this would result in a still larger proportion of the population living as singles in smaller family groups in nonfamily households, and an increasing number and proportion of children living with single parents.

Summary

In the quarter century since 1960 the United States has seen several major changes in living arrangements. They have been affected by shifts in households, family structures, marriages, and divorces. Some of the developments to keep in mind for the future are:

> Households could grow by 20 million from 81 million in 1980 to 101 million in 2000.

Although family households made up 73 percent of all households in 1983, nonfamily households are growing most rapidly.

Married-family households, now 60 percent of all family households, are falling proportionately and projections indicate they could be 52 percent by 1995.

Family households headed by women grew by 72 percent from 1970 to 1983.

In 1983, there were an amazing 19.3 million single-person households, about two-thirds of them occupied by women.

There are now 1.9 million unmarried-couple households, about 4 percent of all couples households.

Household size is continuing to decrease, from 3.33 persons in 1960 to 2.73 persons in 1983.

The majority of households are 1- or 2-person households.

The proportion of 4 persons and over households still exceeds the proportion of singles' households.

Both the number of marriages and the median age of the first marriages has increased steadily since 1960.

About 96 percent of all people marry, the majority remain married and have children, but both men and women are marrying at a later age.

A larger proportion of people will remain single.

Divorces have increased greatly since 1960 but both the number and rate have decreased in the last few years.

Families have become much smaller and although married couples are still 80 percent of all families. Nevertheless, a variety of living arrangements abounds.

The proportion and number of multiearner families has increased.

More than half of all married couples are not multiearner families.

References

Bureau of the Census. 1981. *1980 Census of Population: Characteristics of the Population.* Vol. 1.

———. 1982. *Fertility of American Women: June 1980.* Series P-20, no. 375 (October).

———. 1983a. *Households, Marital Status, and Living Arrangements: March 1983.* Series P-20, no. 382 (July).

———. 1983b. *1980 Census of Population: General, Social, and Economic Characteristics.* Vol. 1.

———. 1984a. *Childspacing among Birth Cohorts of American Women: 1905 to 1959.* Series P-20, no. 385 (April).

———. 1984b. *Homeownership Trends: 1983.* Series H-121 (May).

———. 1984c. *Marital Status and Living Arrangements: March 1983.* Series P-20, no. 389 (July).

———. 1985. *Statistical Abstract of the United States.* 106th ed.

———. 1987. *Commerce News.* March 22.

Department of Housing and Urban Development. 1985. *General Housing Characteristics: 1983 Annual Housing Survey.* Series H-150-83A.

Kelley, Jack. 1985. "One-Parent Homes Soar to 1 in 4." *USA TODAY* (15 May):1.

Taeuber, Cynthia M. and Victor Valdisera. 1986. *Women in the American Economy.* Bureau of the Census. Series P-23, no. 146 (November).

Waldman, Elizabeth. 1983. "Labor Force Statistics from a Family Perspective." *Monthly Labor Review* 106, no. 12 (December):17.

8
Mature Consumers

Introduction

In chapter 1, we commented on the aging and greying of the United States. In chapter 2, we discussed income, including the income of mature households. Now we turn to the age segments that make up mature markets and consider several demographic, income, and life-style dimensions.

The mature market is among the least intensively researched and understood of our age segments (Fisk 1982; Lazer 1985). The available literature seems to contain more unsupported statements and myths than appears to be the case for other groups. Disagreement even exists about the age brackets that comprise the mature market as well as the terms used to describe different segments. Sometimes a 65-and-over classification is used because that age normally marks the age of retirement. Other times a 60-and-over classification is adopted, indicating a decline in physical and mental skills. And in still other cases a 55-and-over classification is used because that represents consumers who have entered the preretirement years. Among the variety of terms used to describe such consumers are seniors, oldsters, older consumers, senior citizens, elderly, old-agers, gerontic population, retirees, and maturites.

The Mature Consumers

Siegel and Davidson used a 55-and-over cutoff to delineate the more mature citizens, but carefully point out some of the important differences that exist among the segments (Siegel & Davidson 1984).

As of 1984, about 50 million Americans were included, 21.3 percent of the population, and their numbers will continue to grow. The 65-and-over market alone will reach about 35 million by the year 2000, accounting for over 21 percent of the population in the year 2030. Future projections are that by the year 2040 the 85-and-over group will number 13 million, over half the current population of Canada (Bureau of the Census 1982). By the year 2050 the average life expectancy will increase to an amazing 80 years.

These projections could be close to the mark because those who will be over 65 in the year 2000 are all living now. Their numbers, however, depend on future mortality and immigration which, in turn, depend on medical advances and world political and economic trends which are difficult, if not impossible, to predict accurately.

The proportion of mature consumers in the United States is lower than is the case in other Western countries such as France, Belgium, Great Britain, Austria, Norway, and Denmark. The proportion of people 65 years and over in them is considerably higher, sometimes reaching 14 percent (Siegel 1981). In West Germany in 1980, the 65-and-over proportion was 14.9 percent; in Sweden it was 15.7 percent. By contrast, some countries in Asia and Africa have a much smaller but growing proportion of elderly. The principal demographic factor that accounts for such variations is fertility, which results in a larger number of young people.

Age alone, of course, does not mean inactivity or that one is "old" and retired. George Burns, at 88, signed a 5-year contract with Caesar's Palace. Segovia is performing in his 90s. Chagall, who died in France in 1985, was active at 97. Ronald Reagan was reelected at age 74. In some activities the older age groups may be among the most prominent and productive participants. Included among these activities are voting, cultural activities, the arts, fine foods, gourmet restaurants, fine wines, luxury travel, and good hotels (Keane 1985).

The Older Segments

Gerontologists often divide the 55-and-over group into four age segments: the olders, 55–64; the elders, 65–74; the aged, 75–84;

and the very old, 85 and over (Bureau of the Census 1982). Marketers have often chosen to use other descriptors to describe mature consumers, depending on the purposes of investigations. Among the terms used are retirees, poor health groups, the younger olders, the seniors, the frail elderly and the old age citizens.

Regardless of the classifications used, two points are evident. First, the mature market is not homogeneous but is comprised of several segments that are vastly different in their market and purchasing behavior (Gelb 1982; Bureau of the Census 1984). In fact, it seems that there may be more intrasegment differentiation than there is intersegment differentiation. That is, the 75-and-over group may comprise very diverse people including some who are vigorous, active, and young, and others who are truly old. Second, current members of the mature market segments are much different in their attitudes, outlook, consumption orientations, and financial means than were their predecessors of even a generation ago (Lazer 1985; Greco 1984). Their attitudes, outlooks, and life-styles are far younger and more youthful than ever (Siegel & Davidson 1984).

Today's 55-year-olds are more like 40- or 45-year-olds of previous generations than their previous 55-year-old cohorts. They feel and act significantly younger than their chronological age might suggest. They invite marketers to appeal to that younger person that exists inside that older person's body. Similar statements may be made about other mature age segments (*American Demographics* 1983; Schewe 1984).

Because of the rapid aging of our population an unduly rapid growth rate is commonly associated with the seniors group, leading to the conclusion that they will become one of the most predominant age classes by the year 2000. But the estimates are that this segment will only include about 35 million people by 2000; the 35–49 age group, by comparison, will total about 63 million people (Robey 1984a).

Projections

Tables 8–1 and 8–2 and figure 8–1 present data on the younger olders, middles, seniors, and very old segments from the present to the year 2050. The population projections in table 8–1 show that

Table 8–1
Estimates of the Mature Market: 1980–95
(millions)

	Younger Olders 55–64	*Middles 65–74*	*Seniors 75–84*	*Very old 85+*	*Total*
1980	22	16	8	2.3	48.3
1985	22	17	9	2.7	50.7
1995	21	19	11	4.1	55.1
% Change 1985–95	−4.5	12	22	52	8.7

Source: Bureau of the Census 1982.

though the number of younger olders, those 55–64, is expected to remain about the same over the 15-year period (1980–95), the other age segments are expected to grow. The fastest growth will occur in the very old, those 85 and over. They also represent the smallest segment.

In 1900, about 4.0 percent of the population, around 3 million people, were 65 and over, less than 10 percent; about 7.1 million were age 55 and over, and only 123,000 were 85 and over. By 1982, however, fully one-fifth of total population was at least 55 years old. About 12 percent, or 27 million, were 65 years and over. Almost 3 million were 85 and over, truly a remarkable shift.

Beyond 1995, the prospects are that the mature market will continue to grow steadily at a rate exceeding the population as a whole for the next 50 years. The most rapid increase will occur between 2010 and 2030. The number of people 65 years and over will increase about 2.5 times. By 2030, they will represent over 21 percent of the population (Bureau of the Census 1984).

By 2010 some 74 million people, about one-quarter of the total population, will be at least 55 years old. One-seventh of our population, or 34.3 million, are projected to be 65 and over. The 75-and-over age group will realize very rapid growth, expanding from 10 million in 1980 to 13.6 million in 1990, and from 17.3 million by 2000 to 19 million in 2010. These people often have special needs that require special attention.

Table 8–2

Growth of the Older Population, Actual and Projected: 1900–2050

(thousands and %)

Year	Total Population, All Ages	55–64		65–74		75–84		85+		65+	
		Number	*%*	*Number*	*%*	*Number*	*%*	*Number*	*%*	*Number*	*%*
1900	76,303	4,009	5.3	2,189	2.9	772	1.0	123	0.2	3,084	4.0
1910	91,972	5,054	5.5	2,793	3.0	989	1.1	167	0.2	3,950	4.3
1920	105,711	6,532	6.2	3,464	3.3	1,259	1.2	210	0.2	4,933	4.7
1930	122,775	8,397	6.8	4,721	3.8	1,641	1.3	272	0.2	6,634	5.4
1940	131,669	10,572	8.0	6,375	4.8	2,278	1.7	365	0.3	9,019	6.8
1950	150,697	13,295	8.8	8,415	5.6	3,278	2.2	577	0.4	12,270	8.1
1960	179,323	15,572	8.7	10,997	6.1	4,633	2.6	929	0.5	16,560	9.2
1970	203,302	18,608	9.2	12,447	6.1	6,124	3.0	1,409	0.7	19,980	9.8
1980	226,505	21,700	9.6	15,578	6.9	7,727	3.4	2,240	1.0	25,544	11.3
1990	249,731	21,090	8.4	18,054	7.2	10,284	4.1	3,461	1.4	31,799	12.7
2000	267,990	23,779	8.9	17,693	6.6	12,207	4.6	5,136	1.9	35,036	13.1
2010	283,141	34,828	12.3	20,279	7.2	12,172	4.3	6,818	2.4	39,269	13.9
2020	296,339	40,243	13.6	29,769	10.0	14,280	4.8	7,337	2.5	51,386	17.3
2030	304,330	33,965	11.2	34,416	11.3	21,128	6.9	8,801	2.9	64,345	21.1
2040	307,952	34,664	11.3	29,168	9.5	24,529	8.0	12,946	4.2	66,643	21.6
2050	308,856	37,276	12.1	30,022	9.7	20,976	6.8	16,063	5.2	67,061	21.7

Source: Bureau of the Census 1982.

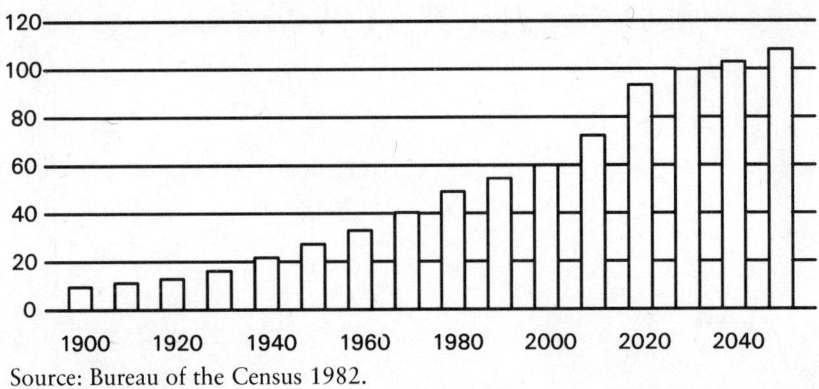

Source: Bureau of the Census 1982.

Figure 8–1. *Population 55 Years and Over: 1900–2050*

Those 85 and over, the true elderly of our society, will grow the fastest of all, doubling from 2.2 million in 1980 to 5.1 million in the year 2000. By the year 2050 they are projected to reach 16 million.

Rapid Aging

The rapidity of the aging is indicated by changes in the median age, which has increased significantly from 28.1 years in 1970 to 30.6 years in 1982. It is projected to reach an amazing 36.3 years in 2000 and continue to increase to 40.8 years in 2030.

Life expectancy is also increasing. It was 74.3 years in 1982, will continue to increase to 76.7 years in 2000 and 81 years in 2080. This compares with a life expectancy of only 49 years in 1900.

A result of these shifts will be a change in the ratio of the working-age population (those 18–64) to the retirement age population, and that creates social and economic concerns. The ratio is projected to realize an unprecedented decline. There were 5.3 people of working age for everyone 65 or older in the United States in 1982, but by the year 2000, the ratio will decline to 4.7. Then it is expected to drop continuously to 2.7 in 2030. This can put a real strain on the working-age population. Hopefully, increases in productivity will serve to handle the demands and to lessen the potential clash between the younger working-age population and those who are retired.

The other side of the aging picture, of course, is the relative and absolute decline of the younger adults, the 18–24-year-olds. They provided the engine for growth in the later 1960s and during the 1970s. Now, they are at an all time high of 30 million. But by 1995 they will have a sharp drop to about 23 million, while the elder population will grow. Then, beyond 2000 they will have but slow growth to 24.5 million in 2000 and 28 million in 2010.

Life-styles

Considering each of the sectors from a life-style perspective, today's 55–64-year-olds, when compared with those of the 1940s and 1950s, can hardly be considered olders, based on their activities, interests, outlooks, and life-styles (Cruikshank 1982). They are keenly interested in maintaining their youthful appearance and comprise prime markets for a wide variety of items ranging from cosmetic surgery and diets to sports and exercise equipment. They think younger than their counterparts of previous generations. The younger olders lead very active lives and have more of an orientation of working to live, rather than the living to work orientation of their parents. An increasing number are, in fact, taking earlier retirement, controlling more of their time, moving into totally new careers, as well as into part-time jobs. They are often more concerned with added discretionary time rather than additional discretionary income. They have the greatest per-capita income of all age segments and may suffer from a poverty of time (Gelb 1982; Lazer 1985; Schewe 1984).

The middle olders, the 65–74-year-old age group, also resemble far younger people in their attitude, education, income, use of leisure, time, health, and marital status. They are well into their retirement years and a decreasing proportion of them continue to work, at least part time. the labor-force participation rates for all men 65 and over decreased from 26.8 percent in 1970 to 16.3 percent in 1984, while that for all women 65 and over declined from 9.7 percent to 7.5 percent. Their family incomes, surprisingly, are about 90 percent of the income of all families (Bureau of the Census

1982). They are especially oriented to personal maintenance and support products and services, such as nutrition, health, medical, and beauty aids. They are interested in lighter and healthier foods, skin care and pharmaceutical products, and a diversity of products that ease pain and promote the ready performance of everyday physical activities. While the 65-and-older group historically spent more on food at home, rather than away from home, that pattern now seems to be shifting as the middle olders comprise a growing market for restaurants and catering activities. Also, a greater proportion of the services formerly handled from the home are now being performed by others, including lawn care, snow removal, and a spectrum of household maintenance functions and daily chores.

The 75–84-year-olds, the seniors, tend to resemble the oft-held image of the previous 65-and-over group, "those old-age consumers." For them health is often a problem and mobility tends to be more limited. Many are concerned about financial security, but others, as we shall see, have substantial assets, such as fully paid homes. The seniors are often lonesome, and may be more oriented to their extended families in their expenditures. Some require extensive health-care services and special care facilities.

The 85-and-over age group are the true elderly, sometimes referred to as the frail elderly of our society. Interestingly enough, they may be in a unique position of knowing four or five generations of a family, a historical first, and some may have worked for 50 to 60 years. They are far different in their purchasing decisions and behavior from other mature market segments because most are not as independent, often requiring some support services or special health care to carry on. Many lack mobility and require regular medical and hospital care. They portend a vast and growing market for many supportive health, medical, and living services. They are projected to grow in numbers from about 2.25 million in 1980 to over 16 million in 2050. But their wants and needs are not at all well understood.

Two of the most important factors affecting buyer behavior and consumption habits and patterns of older consumers are rarely covered by the marketing literature. One is whether or not a consumer's mate is still alive and/or whether a couple is living together. The second relates to health, particularly whether or not the consumers are still fairly mobile, both physically and psychologically, and have ready access to transportation. Both factors make a big difference in shopping and consumption patterns and are significant determinants worth researching for life-style purposes.

A few other life-style–related characteristics revealed by 1982 and 1983 statistics are:

> About five-sixths of all men 65 and over live in a family setting, with three-fourths being married and living with their wives. But for women 65 and over the situation is different for they are more likely to be widowed than married, and make up most of the 7 million 65-and-over group living alone.
>
> The current education gap between the elderly and their younger counterparts will narrow significantly after 1995 because of the education thrust that occurred after World War II, and increased immigration, which comprised a higher proportion of better-educated foreign born.
>
> The proportion of males aged 65 and over who are working, or looking for work, has been dropping rapidly for over 30 years from 50 percent in 1950 to 18.4 percent in 1980. A similar trend, but at a slower rate, occurs for the 50–64 age segment. After the age 70 the proportion declines rapidly.
>
> For women, however, the trend is different, because women 55–64 increasingly have been joining the work force, growing from 27 percent of the work force in 1950 to 42 percent in 1980. Although the 65-and-over women's work force has held steady at about 10 percent, women are increasingly choosing to work part time.

Mature Markets and Poverty

To some observers, older households are considered as synonymous with poor households, representing rather limited markets for discretionary and luxury items. Sometimes a picture of the 65-and-over sector that emerges is that most of them live at the poverty level, devoid of assets and income, in inadequate housing, unable to afford needed medical help, and being very dependent on government handouts. But such portraits are most misleading, for an analysis of income data indicates that many mature consumers have the incomes to indulge themselves to a much greater extent than was the case previously.

Today's elderly, in reality, are no more likely to be poor than the nonaged, for the elderly have a poverty rate only slightly above that of the general population. Elderly married couples are usually better off than widows and unmarrieds, so that there are pockets of poverty among elderly people living alone, particularly women and elderly minorities. As for official poverty status, when other benefits are considered, the numbers of mature consumers below poverty drop significantly and some analysts argue that the elderly have higher per-capita incomes than the population at large (Linden, Green & Coder no date; Allan 1984).

There exists a retirement elite, people who have not suffered at all in retirement. About one-third of the people 85 and older have household incomes at least twice as high as the federal poverty level. In Hawaii, the proportion is 46 percent. Over 50 percent of the 85-and-over group own their own homes. Relative to other groups the incomes of the elderly have actually increased over the 1970s. They have a much higher proportion of discretionary income and account for a much higher proportion of family purchasing decisions than their numbers suggest (Hurd & Shoven 1982).

Income alone does not indicate the economic well-being of older consumers nor is it a good indicator of the market potential they represent.

> The census definition of income includes money only; important noncash income such as food stamps, or employer-provided health care, is not counted.
>
> Elderly consumers often have substantial assets, such as homes or investments, but receive little income. About 75 percent of those 65 and over own their own homes, with 84 percent of them being owned free and clear (Bureau of the Census 1984).
>
> Elderly consumers are often the recipients of a variety of noncash benefits.

> Elderly consumers, like younger consumers, may be part of the underground economy working for cash payments "off the books."
>
> Many elderly households are made up of a single person, largely widows and widowers, and a few who were never married or are divorced. In 1980, only 38 percent of the women 65 and over were wives living in married-couple households. From 1970 to 1980, the number of women 65 and over living alone increased to 5.8 million. There were 1.5 million men who lived alone in 1980.

At one extreme, an elderly couple with $500,000 in assets could be receiving less than $6,000 a year in income and would then be classified as poor. Yet, we should also note that a large proportion of elderly households are indeed poor, for incomes tend to peak late in the middle years and are considerably lower for those 65 and over. But, in the last decade the incomes of elderly families have converged with those of all families. The majority of elderly people are not poor, and are not as likely to be poor as are younger people. Estimates of the poor in 1983 for those 65 and over was 12 percent compared with 14 percent for those under 65. For those less than 15 years of age the proportion was 22 percent, and for 15–24 years it was 17 percent.

Bearing these caveats in mind we shall investigate household income projections and their implications to 1995. All household income projections are given in 1980 dollars, and are based on an assumed conservative 1.5 percent annual income growth rate, a far lower rate than the 2.5 to 3.0 percent of previous decades.

For our analysis the mature market is subdivided into two main segments: the 55–64 age sector, the preretirement phase, and the 65-and-over sector, the retirement group. Although this tends to blur some distinctions and emphasizes homogeneity, the distortions engendered are not believed to be great. In 1982, the 75-and-over age group made up less than 5 percent of the total population; the 85-and-over group was only about 1 percent. First, we shall compare the incomes of mature versus younger households. Then we shall briefly investigate incomes of all households and then husband–wife households.

Mature versus Younger Households

When incomes of mature markets are compared with those of younger market segments, the general pattern is that income tends to increase until about age 55 and then declines when a larger number of people begin to retire. As age increases beyond 55, income declines steadily, although a growing minority manage to maintain relatively high and even increasing incomes in their later years.

Significant differences exist between the incomes of aging men and those of aging women. Income declines associated with aging begin at both a lower age for women than for men (50 versus 55) and at lower income levels. Actual incomes received by older populations are more associated with such factors as health, the ability to continue working, education, survival of spouses, pension plans, and other retirement provisions such as IRAs, rather than just age or sex per se.

Mature families also tend to be smaller than their younger family counterparts. When size is considered, the income of elderly families is about 90 percent of that of all families, and the financial burdens may be less, although medical expenditures increase disproportionately. As a result, the income of 65-and-over married couples tends to approach that of their young married sons and daughters. The income for elderly people not living with families, such as the divorced or widowed persons, is indeed lower.

Understandably, older people earning low incomes tend to feel less secure than their younger counterparts earning the same incomes. The younger earners can look forward to increasing their future incomes. This feeling of insecurity on the part of mature workers can be an important consideration in consumer expenditures.

Of the mature market segments, single women over 65 have the lowest incomes and are the most likely to be poor. But where people 65 years of age and over work full time (a larger proportion of elderly mature singles are not fully employed), their incomes until age 70 tend to be quite similar to the incomes of the younger single people.

An important difference between the present 65-and-over households as compared with both younger households, and future older households, relates to education. Data in 1983 revealed that less than 10 percent of the elderly population attended 4 or more years of college and about 44 percent attended high school. The figures are even lower for those 75 and over. But this educational gap will narrow in the future and the rising educational levels of older consumers could well be accompanied by rising incomes. Then the gap in the purchasing ability of younger and older households could well shrink.

The work experience of members of current 65-and-over households occurred when relatively poor pensions and medical benefits existed as compared with the benefits of those who are in the laborforce today and will be retiring after 2000. The future picture is thus expected to be brighter. Also, it could well be that a larger proportion of future elderly household income will come from earnings, property income, and private pensions, with Social Security declining in importance as a retirement income source for many.

Mature Household Incomes: 1980–95

Tables 8–3 and 8–4 present data on income projections for mature households based on an assumed 1.5 percent annual growth rate.

The total number of 55–64 households is expected to decrease slightly over the period. Whereas the number of 65-and-over households will increase by a startling 52 million. Both segments are projected to have a very high concentration of both under-$10,000 and $10,000 to $19,999 households.

The greatest concentration of 55–64 year old households both in 1980 and 1995 is in the $10,000–$19,999 income bracket. The largest proportionate shift, as is shown in table 8–4, occurs in the $50,000-and-over households which almost doubles, although the base is small. The $35,000-and-over households increase, and the under $25,000 households decrease, but, nevertheless, about 50 percent of the 55–64 households have incomes under $25,000.

Among the 65-and-over households the largest concentration definitely remains in the under-$10,000 income category, which accounts for over 55 percent of 1980, and 47 percent of 1995 households. The 65-and-over households with incomes under $20,000 do

Table 8–3
Mature Household Income: 1980 and 1995
(in multiples of 100,000 households)

	55–64 Households (Preretirement)		*65+ Households (Senior Citizens)*	
Income	*1980*	*1995*	*1980*	*1995*
Under $10,000	30	22	89	100
$10,000–$19,999	32	26	43	63
$20,000–$24,999	14	12	9	15
$25,000–$34,999	21	21	10	16
$35,000–$49,999	17	21	6	11
$50,000+	11	20	4	8
Total	125	122	161	213

Note: Data are based on the author's projections, using the methodology described in chapter 2.

make up over 82 percent and 76 percent of the 1980 and 1995 totals, respectively. They account for over 42 percent of all the under-$10,000 households and 63 percent of the $10,000–$19,999 units. The data also indicate that the $25,000-and-over elderly households will grow by about 5 million with 35 percent in this bracket.

Considering income only, these households would appear to be the less fortunate households, the poorer market segments, denoting poverty amidst growing widespread household affluence. Yet, as we have noted, great caution must be exercised in drawing conclusions about their purchasing power. The 65-and-over households include a very high concentration of singles, whether widows, widowers or, never married. Their obligations are different, other benefits are received, and income for them need not equate with economic well-being.

Some of the elderly have simply chosen to work less and realize lower incomes, but have more leisure time. For most, housing is a very important asset and about 75 percent of all the households they maintained in 1980 were owner occupied. One half of these

Table 8–4
Percentage Changes in Mature Household Income: 1980 and 1995

	Preretirement (55–64)		*Senior Citizens (65+)*	
Income	*1980*	*1995*	*1980*	*1995*
Under $10,000	24.02	18.23	55.54	47.05
$10,000–$19,999	25.33	21.25	26.78	29.68
$20,000–$24,999	11.21	10.04	5.79	6.92
$25,000–$34,999	16.96	16.97	6.02	7.57
$35,000–$49,999	13.77	17.11	3.54	5.02
$50,000+	8.70	16.38	2.33	3.77

Note: Data are based on the author's projections, using the methodology described in chapter 2.

households were owned free and clear, and of all free-and-clear homes, two-thirds are maintained by the 65 and over segment.

For the mature population the burdens of the heavy costs of home financing are eased, as are childrearing expenses, many work-related expenses, home furnishings expenditures, and possessions that have already been paid for. Also, family and financial burdens are greatly reduced, there is little need to save for the future, and older members of the mature segment receive various benefits such as indexing of some retirement incomes. An offset for some of them are unduly large medical expenditures.

The Mature Husband–Wife Households

When husband–wife household incomes are considered, the income picture is even rosier, as is shown in tables 8–5 and 8–6. Still, marked differences exist in the income patterns of 55–64 and 65-and-over households.

From 1980 to 1995, the 55–64-year-old households will realize significant income gains, with the largest income segment shifting from the $10,000–$19,999 category to the $35,000–$49,999 category. In 1995, about two-thirds of the 55–64 households are pro-

Table 8–5
Mature Husband–Wife Household Incomes: 1980 and 1995
(in multiples of 100,000 households)

	1980		*1995*	
Income	*55–64*	*65+*	*55–64*	*65+*
Under $10,000	10	24	6	20
$10,000–$19,999	19	27	14	37
$20,000–$24,999	10	6	8	10
$25,000–$34,999	17	7	15	11
$35,000–$49,999	16	4	18	8
$50,000+	10	3	18	6
Total	82	71	79	92

Note: Data are based on the author's projections, using the methodology described in chapter 2.

Table 8–6
Percentage Changes in Mature Husband–Wife Household Incomes: 1980 and 1995

	Preretirement (55–64)		*Senior Citizens (65+)*	
Income	*1980*	*1995*	*1980*	*1995*
Under $10,000	11.63	7.77	34.43	22.14
$10,000–$19,999	23.56	17.27	37.72	40.15
$20,000–$24,999	12.69	10.35	8.54	10.37
$25,000–$34,999	21.04	19.26	9.47	12.09
$35,000–$49,999	18.85	22.32	5.87	8.57
$50,000+	12.23	23.04	3.98	6.69

Note: Data are based on the author's projections, using the methodology described in chapter 2.

jected to be in the $25,000-and-over category and a great reduction will occur in the under-$25,000 segment.

Because the 55–64 husband–wife households are usually relatively free of many of the previously heavy financial burdens associated with childrearing, housing, and furnishing, they may become more inclined to spend on themselves. And though their incomes are not nearly as high as incomes of middle-aged consumers, nevertheless they represent attractive market opportunities, for they have a large proportion of discretionary income.

The income picture for the 65-and-over husband–wife households is different. Their income has been affected by the one-time catch-up increase in Social Security of the 1970s and the cost of living adjustments from 1975 on. By 1995, over 62 percent of them are projected to remain in the $20,000-and-under bracket with almost three-fourths in the under-$25,000 categories. These retirement households make up about two-thirds of all the under-$10,000 category and 42 percent of the $10,000–$19,999 husband–wife households category. Only 15 percent of them are projected to be in the $35,000-and-over category. The $10,000–$19,999 bracket will likely remain the largest income segment, followed by the under-$10,000 households. But, as was mentioned before, income alone does not indicate their economic well-being.

Importance of Mature Consumers

The market impact of the mature consumers is far greater than their total numbers suggest, for the 55-and-over age group now accounts for purchasing decisions in about one-third of the family units, and their influence will continue to increase (*New York Times* 1982). The proportion of households with spendable discretionary income, and the per-capita spendable discretionary income for households over 50 is greater than that of households 49 and under (Linden, Green & Coder no date). The mature households control much of the discretionary income, yet we do not know a great deal about their purchasing behavior and expenditure patterns.

Married couples 55 and over are relatively free of many previous financial burdens associated with establishing a home and family, and childrearing. Many of the 55-and-over consumers are well able to afford more luxurious life-styles than many actually enjoy. And when the assets of mature consumers are translated into regular income streams by such financial devices as the reverse mortgage, mature consumers have the money to enjoy their wealth.

Also, those 65 and over receive various benefits and allowances. Reliable estimates of the cash value of benefits received by the 65-and-over group are both difficult to derive and substantiate. Estimates have been made and when they are considered, the number of elderly households below the poverty line declines significantly and some estimates calculate that they decrease from 15 percent to 10 percent of all households (Siegel & Davidson 1984).

Regionally, mature households of three sunbelt states (Arizona, California, and Florida) and New York have a substantial number of well-to-do retirees. Many of the mature well-to-do have immigrated from other states. Overall, the state of Florida has the largest population in the 65-and-over group, 17.3 percent; California has the largest number, 2.6 million. In 1981, seven states (Florida, California, New York, Pennsylvania, Texas, Illinois, and Ohio) were estimated to have over one million people 65 and over (Bureau of the Census 1982).

Consumption Patterns

The consumption patterns and purchasing behavior of mature consumers are the topic of much conjecture in the literature that seems to make sense but often lacks statistical evidence. Some are in partial conflict with other published statements. It has been noted, for example, that mature consumers are more cautious in their purchases and shrewder as comparison shoppers, but they are also characterized as being more set in their purchase patterns, and more brand loyal. They are more susceptible to social influences and are also more likely to be individualistic and express themselves without caring what the neighbors think. They are described as being more likely to buy nationally advertised brands, and at the same time as being more likely to seek the best deal. They are seen as partial to large chains and also as preferring service stores. We are

told that they are more likely to read newspap
well informed. And, though they are respons
and services, they are described as not as like.
selves. All of the above could be true of course
mature population segments, but as generalizations
somewhat, and are usually lacking in hard data. Such co
therefore, may be open to question and present fine re
opportunities.

Some observers note that mature consumers are hampered in their consumption behavior by difficult experiences suffered during the Great Depression of the 1930s, and the scarcities encountered during World War II. They have been described as hesitant consumers who live more cautiously and frugally than need be, denying rather than indulging themselves. At the same time, other observers report that mature consumers are less concerned with leaving an inheritance for their families and are now enjoying their wealth and money. They note a major transition in purchasing behavior with mature consumers adopting a more hedonistic approach to life and spending more freely.

The life-styles and purchasing behavior of mature consumers may be more directly related to their health, independence, and self-sufficiency than to other purchase-related factors. The degree of self-sufficiency comprises a spectrum. At one extreme are consumers who are totally self-sufficient physically, psychologically, and economically. At the other are those who are totally dependent. In between are various gradations where mature consumers might be mainly self-sufficient or largely dependent on others, and such factors greatly affect market opportunities.

Among the conjectures about buyer behavior of mature consumers suggested by the literature are the following (Greco 1984; Allan 1984; Lazer 1984):

1. Mature consumers differ from other consumers in their sources of information.
2. Mature consumers differ from younger consumers in methods of processing information and accepting new products.

3. Mature consumers are heavy users of television and of newspapers and therefore can be reached by communications media.
4. Shopping is a source of pleasure rather than a chore for many older consumers; it is a major part of their life-style.
5. Those consumers who were socially and physically active in their younger years remains so in their later years.
6. Mature women no longer live their lives mainly through their families and children, but live for themselves.
7. The purchase behavior of mature consumers who live alone is far different than it is for those who live with mates.
8. Mature consumers are not always the least active consumers.
9. There is probably a greater difference in buyer behavior within an elderly age category than there is between age categories. Thus, some 64-year-olds may be more like 80-year-olds and vice versa.

Table 8–7 shows a comparison of expenditure patterns of youthful and mature households in 1984 derived from census data (Bureau of the Census 1985). A careful reading will indicate that mature consumers spend less for food (but have smaller-sized families), shelter, household operations, major and small appliances, and clothing, and in general are reasonably well off in terms of the necessities of life. They spend considerably less for transportation and on operating, maintaining, financing, and repairing cars. As expected they dramatically outspend younger consumers for health care—insurance, medicines, and medical supplies. Expenditures on entertainment, television, radio and sound equipment are lower; those for newspapers and personal care are higher. The latter are significantly higher for mature women as compared with their younger counterparts. Contributions to both religious and political organizations and charities are also higher.

The above indicates the variety of information about expenditures that is available. The data, however are aggregated, which can

Table 8–7
Average Consumer Expenditure Patterns, 1984: Comparison of Households of Mature and Youthful Consumers

	Youthful Consumer Households (25 to 54)	*All Consumer Households (25 to 85+)*	*Mature Consumer Households (55 to 85+)*
Total Expenditures[a]	$22,828	$20,862	$17,144
Expenditure categories	19,938	18,228	14,996
Food	3,481	3,280	2,900
Food at home	2,391	2,300	2,129
Grocery stores	2,235	2,164	2,029
Convenience stores	155	136	99
Food away from home	1,090	980	772
Alcoholic beverages	340	286	184
Housing	6,921	6,284	5,079
Shelter	4,010	3,494	2,520
Owned dwellings	2,352	2,066	1,526
Rented dwellings	1,299	1,071	641
Fuel, utilities, and public services	1,634	1,638	1,645
Household operations	338	315	275
Domestic services	280	252	199
Housekeeping services	52	62	80
Other household services	56	63	76
Housefurnishings and equipment	941	837	640
Furniture	319	270	178
Major appliances	151	141	123
Small appliances/miscellaneous	67	62	53
Miscellaneous household equipment	260	229	169
Apparel	1,276	1,107	788
Males, 2 and over	343	285	177
Females, 2 and over	495	447	356
Transportation	4,678	4,264	3,226
Vehicle purchases	2,113	1,813	1,247
Vehicles finance charges	266	213	113
Gasoline and motor oil	1,172	1,058	842
Maintenance and repairs	490	439	344
Health care[a]	715	902	1,256
Health insurance	177	291	507
Medical services	427	454	504
Medicines and medical supplies	110	157	245

Table 8-7 continued

	Youthful Consumer Households (25 to 54)	*All Consumer Households (25 to 85+)*	*Mature Consumer Households (55 to 85+)*
Entertainment	$1,131	$973	$674
Fees and admissions	354	313	238
Televisions	253	219	154
Radios and sound equipment	112	91	50
Other entertainment supplies and equipment	413	350	233
Personal care	187	192	203
Electric personal care appliances	5	5	3
Personal services for females	106	121	150
Personal services for males	75	66	49
Reading	137	132	122
Newspapers	55	61	71
Magazines/periodicals	35	33	28
Book clubs	10	9	7
Encyclopedias/other reference books	5	3	1
Education	360	286	147
Elementary and high schools	63	46	15
Colleges and universities	212	175	105
Other schools	20	16	10
Tobacco and smoking supplies	249	227	185
Miscellaneous	329	295	232
Contributions	661	706	791
Charities	67	73	83
Churches/religious organizations	235	259	303
Educational organizations	15	13	10
Political	5	7	12
Personal insurance	2,230	1,928	1,357
Life, endowments, annuities, etc.	301	300	297
Retirement/pensions, Social Security	1,929	1,628	1,060

Source: Lazer and Shaw 1986.

[a]Some subcategories may not sum to category total due to the omission of detailed items from total.

obscure patterns; one cannot tell whether purchases are made for one's own use or for gifts. Additional research and analysis will aid in generating greater understanding about living standards and the quality of life of mature consumers (Lazer and Shaw 1987).

Product and Service Propositions

Various propositions can be developed from findings about products and services. The following are included:

1. Even the most obvious product and service needs of mature consumers are only now being considered, including low-salt, and low-cholesterol foods; menus featuring baked and broiled fish and poultry rather than fried foods; decaffeinated beverages; a variety of home-care services; telephone books in large print; buildings and transportation to accommodate wheelchairs; telephones for the hard of hearing; clothing designs that eliminate buttons; and packages that open easily. In fact, we do not seem to know much about the preferences of the elderly, although articles point out that they have a passion for travel. No data are given on how they differ from other consumers, but such data could exist in the proprietary form.
2. It may be that the greatest potential is not in products designed for the elderly, but in getting the elderly to spend more freely on products currently being sold to other markets. The elderly may tend to resist being singled out for attention and may refuse to "buy old."
3. The elderly may use products already on the market for different purposes. For example, video games that the young use for entertainment can sharpen the motor and visual skills of the elders. Home retailing, a convenience for others, may be a psychological and physical necessity for some of the elderly. Especially designed TV, for example, may not merely be entertainment and a means of diversion, but a real boon for the hearing impaired, connecting them with the outside world via telex and video shopping.

4. Effective advertising appeals directed at elderly consumers are merely an extension of appeals used for other markets.
5. Many older consumers simply make do with the products they already have and therefore spend less than they can comfortably afford.
6. Because older consumers do not anticipate buying some durable products again, they may be more interested in quality, durability, and service.
7. Are the fashion leaders and innovators among the elderly merely an extension of their younger counterparts, or are other attributes important?

Summary

Myths abound about the 55-and-over market (the "mature market"), which comprises 50 million citizens. It is a heterogeneous market made up of four distinct segments: the younger olders, the middle group, the senior sector, and the very old. The segments differ in attitudes, consumption orientations, financial means, and life-styles even from their predecessors of a generation ago. Overall, they are the fastest growing age sector. By 2030, the 65-and-over sector alone will account for over 21 percent of the U.S. population.

Contrary to public belief, mature consumers are no more likely to be poor than are younger consumers. They have considerably higher discretionary incomes than any other age group and have the time to enjoy shopping and consumption. Yet their behavior is conditioned by some unique events, such as the Great Depression and World War II. These events have made them overly conservative and cautious in their expenditures. These people have the incomes to indulge themselves to a greater extent than they actually do.

Two factors that have great impact on purchasing behavior are whether or not a mate is still alive and if the couple is living together, and whether they are physically and psychologically mobile.

Demographic projections comparing 1980 with 1995, using a zero population growth rate, indicate that the younger olders (55–64) are expected to remain about the same; the middles (65–74), seniors (75–84), and very old (85+) will grow significantly. The very old will grow by 50 percent.

The 55–64-year-olds can hardly be considered old based on activities, outlooks, interests, and life-styles. They are keenly interested in youthful appearances and they create prime markets for a variety of products and services. These services range from cosmetic surgery to diets and exercise equipment. They are retiring earlier and are often more interested in discretionary time than in discretionary income.

The middle olders, though well into their retirement years, are also young at heart. They are oriented toward personal maintenance and support products and services, such as nutrition, health, medical, and beauty aids. They are into lighter and healthier food, skin-care products, pharmaceuticals, and items that reduce pain and increase mobility.

The seniors tend to resemble the oft-held image of "old-age consumers." Health is often a problem and mobility tends to decrease. They are often lonely and are more oriented towards their extended families in their expenditures.

The 85-and-over are the true elderly, the very old. They are far different in their purchasing behavior from other mature consumers. They are not as independent, and often require support services or special health care to carry on. They may be in the position of knowing four or five generations of a family—a historical first. They tend to spend on the extended family rather than on themselves.

By 1995, significantly larger proportions of mature households will have incomes in the $25,000-and-over and $50,000-and-over ranges, in 1980 dollars. Similarly, the proportions in the lower income categories will decline. Incomes of mature consumers, however, cannot be equated with economic well-being for they exclude such considerations as wealth, assets, and financial obligations. When these are factored in, it is evident that mature consumers comprise very lucrative markets. We are in the midst of a major transition in which people may lead productive working lives for 60–80 years, have two generations of parents to support, and enjoy much better health well into old age. Marketers have opportunities to develop and test hypotheses about reactions of mature consumers to various products and services, to promotional approaches, and to various distribution channels. They are challenged to debunk some of the mature-market myths. Marketing to the mature market does not mean marketing to the elderly, and the new consumer market slogan may be that life begins at 65, not at 40.

References

American Demographics. 1983. "Selling the Seniors" (February):14.

Bureau of the Census. 1979. "Consequences of Changing U.S. Population: Demographics of Aging." *Current Population Reports*. Series P-23, no. 78 (January).

———. 1982. "Projections of the Population of the United States: 1982 to 2080." *Current Population Reports*. Series P-25, no. 922 (November).

———. 1984. "Projections of the Population of the United States by Age, Sex, and Race: 1983 to 2080." *Current Population Reports*. Series P-25, no. 952.

———. 1985. Data are derived from an analysis of 1984 Consumer Expenditure Survey data tapes.

Cruikshank, G. 1982. "The Wellderly." *Across the Board* (June):72.

Fareed, A. E., and G. D. Riggs. 1982. "Old–Young Differences in Consumer Expenditure Patterns." *Journal of Consumer Affairs* (Summer):152.

Fisk, George. 1982. "Marketing Implications of an Aging Workforce." *The Collegiate Forum* (Fall):18.

Gelb, B. D. 1982. "Discovering the 65+ Consumer." *Business Horizons* (May–June):42.

Greco, Alan J. 1984. "Overlooked Senior Citizen Market Lends Itself Well to a Segmentation Approach." *Marketing News* (27 April):7.

Hurd, M., and J. B. Shoven. 1982. "Real Income and Wealth of the Elderly." *American Economic Review* (May):314.

Keane, John G. 1985. Unpublished address, Florida Atlantic University (April).

Lambert, Z. V. 1979. *Lifetime Allocation of Work and Income: Essays in the Economics of Aging*. Durham, N.C.: Duke University Press.

Lazer, William. 1984. "How Rising Affluence Will Reshape Markets." *American Demographics* (February):17.

———. 1985. "Inside the Mature Market." *American Demographics* (March): 23–25; 48–49.

———. 1986. "Dimensions of the Mature Market." *The Journal of Consumer Behavior* Vol. 3, no. 3 (Summer).

———, and Eric H. Shaw. 1987. "Expenditure Patterns of Mature Consumers and Quality of Life Issues." Unpublished paper. American Marketing Association, Marketing Theory Conference, San Antonio, Texas (February).

Linden, Fabian, Gorden W. Green, Jr., and John F. Coder. No date. *A Marketer's*

Guide to Discretionary Income. Consumer Research Center and Bureau of the Census.

Mason, J. B., and B. Smith. 1973. "An Exploratory Note on the Shopping Behavior of the Low Income Senior Citizen." *Journal of Consumer Affairs* (Summer).

New York Times. 1982. "How Poor Are the Elderly?" (19 December):4F.

Robey, Bryant. 1984a. "Entering Middle-Age." *American Demographics* (February):4.

———. 1984b. "On Demographics." *American Demographics* (March):11.

Schewe, Charles D. 1984. "Research Dispels Myths about Elderly, Suggested Marketing Opportunities." *Marketing News* (25 May):12.

Siegel, Jacob S. 1981. "Demographic Background for International Gerontological Studies." *Journal of Gerontology* 36, no. 1 (January):93–102.

———, and Maria Davidson. 1984. "Demographic and Socioeconomic Aspects of Aging in the United States." *Current Population Reports.* Series P-23, no. 138 (August). Bureau of the Census.

Wall Street Journal. 1986. "New Study Looks at the State of Nation's 'Old-Age Citizens'" (5 August):31.

9
The New Consumers

The Changing Order

The U.S. marketplace is now governed by the appearance of a new breed of consumers. Previously consumers were affected by such factors as the growth of the smokestack industries, U.S. dominance of world markets, the growing value of the U.S. dollar, and the acceptance of the Protestant ethic, all of which are giving way. New societal and economic forces are in place and are joined by new consumer orientations and behavioral determinants that prescribe many of the dimensions of the new consumers.

"We are now facing far different consumers—consumers that respond in a different manner than they did in the 1970s," remarked a marketing vice president of a large consumer products manufacturing company, as he reflected on some recent market changes and their impact on the development of long-run strategic plans. He is correct: the consumers of the 1980s are not clones of those of the 1960s and 1970s, but are indeed markedly different. We shall explore four sets of forces shaping future consumer marketplace reactions.

What is new about U.S. consumers? Why and how are they different? How do factors shaping consumption differ? What broad trends are affecting and influencing them? In this chapter we shall explore various dimensions of such questions.

We shall consider two broad and general groups of forces, namely, societal trends and economic shifts, and two groups that more directly influence consumers, namely consumer orientations and behavioral determinants.

Societal Shifts

In *The Next Economy,* Hawken noted that "business success comes from the ability to perceive wants and needs and that perception depends acutely on sensitivity to people and their environment" (Hawken 1983, p. 79). Some of the major shifts in our broader societal environments are summarized in table 9–1.

As has been well documented, ours is an economy in transition. We are moving rapidly from an industrial society with its smoke-stack industries and human power inputs to an information society, with its computers, automation, robotics, and high-tech emphasis. In the process our production and distribution are becoming far less centralized and concentrated; there is a great pull towards decentralization and to smaller centers of production in order to bring greater decision authority near the marketplace. Our massive, inflexible production systems are giving way to more flexible and adaptable systems that can shift more readily to meet changing market demands.

Table 9–1
Societal Trends

From	*To*
Industrial society	Information society
Centralization	Decentralization
Mass and inflexibility	Flexibility and adaptation
Human labor	Automation
Sales, profits, production	Humans
Racism/sexism	Ageism
Top-down management	Bottom-up management
Bigness	Appropriate scale
"Company" boards	Outside boards
Privacy	Community
Representative democracy	Participative democracy
Party politics	Issue politics
Nationalism	Worldism
Increasing scarcity and limits to growth	Increasing abundance and boundaries

Past company orientations that focus almost totally on sales, profits, and production data, the so-called "bottom line," are being tempered by far greater concern for human resources—for people. The realization that organizations are made up of people and not numbers is becoming more prevalent, resulting in changes in management styles such as a shift from top-down to bottom-up management, involving all levels in the decision-making process. The past belief that most of the brains and ability in a company are at the top of the management hierarchy is giving way.

Discrimination based on race and sex certainly has not disappeared, but it is now being tempered. Future discrimination may shift from sexism and racism to ageism. This could evolve after the turn of the century as a result of our maturing population, with the growing number of people 55 and over in the labor force accompanied by a challenge of younger workers for jobs, promotion, and benefits.

The previous business orientation held that bigger is better, and companies competed avidly to become the largest in their industry, or to achieve the largest market share or the greatest sales volume. The movement now is to reach an appropriate scale, a scale necessary for efficiency, or for aggressive competition, rather than merely striving to become big for the sake of bigness.

Boards of directors comprised almost exclusively of "company people" are now branching out to encompass outside board members, including consumer and minority representatives who can bring a more dispassionate perspective to corporations. And the previous notion that company decisions and policies are private matters of concern to the company only is being replaced by the perception that community interests are involved and that businesses must take them into consideration in their plans and decisions.

Representative democracy, where chosen or elected representatives made decisions for their constituents, is being altered by an emphasis on participative democracy where those concerned participate actively in decisions and actions. As a result, party politics are being altered by the appearance of issue politics where people concerned with an issue act in consort, regardless of political party affiliations or beliefs.

Regardless of the current spotlight on protectionism and trade, U.S. society is increasingly moving away from a perspective of nationalism to a recognition of worldism. There is recognition of the global impact on business of our nation's actions in conjunction with those of other nations. The outlook in an information economy shifts from national markets and a regional or local market perspective to global markets, multinational corporations, world trade, and competition. The interrelationships and global impact among the strategies and decisions of countries and regions are considered.

Recognition has been given in the recent past to considerations of the limits to growth, business impact on environments, the existence of some world shortages in resources, and the necessity of curbing reckless expansion. We are more cognizant of the possibility of some scarcities and the pollution of environments. Yet, overall many nations are actually shifting from relative scarcity to increasing abundance. Most industrial nations are expanding and are better off now than they were previously, although problems will continue to persist, and environmental boundaries may raise barriers to continuing rapid growth.

These general environmental shifts affect consumers, their dreams and aspirations, how they live and what they buy. Though they are not as direct in their influences as consumption-shaping factors, they should not be ignored, for they do make real differences. Such forces as worldism, automation, abundance, appropriate scale, and decentralization alter the standards of living and expectations of the new breed of consumers.

Economic Shifts

Our economy is in the throes of a major transition from an industrial to a postindustrial or information economy. Some of the major changes that will occur in the shift from the changing consumer marketplace responses are highlighted in table 9–2.

The industrial economy emphasized the creation of production utilities and focused on developing producer-friendly processes that enhanced speed of production, lower costs, the acceptance of a certain proportion of defects, and in general, forced consumers to ad-

Table 9–2
Economic Shifts

From	*To*
Industrial Economy	*Information Economy*
Production utility	Consumption utility
Producer friendly	User friendly
Quantity	Quality
Defects	Service
Consumers adjust	Producers adjust
	Modules
	Zero defects
Mass	Differentiation
Homogenization	Segments
Uniformity	Customize and individualize
Mass production	Flexible production
Growth	Stability
Expansion	Contraction
Scale	Divest
Chains	Smaller size
Accumulate	Share
Amass resources	Mutuality of interests
Dominate	Cooperation
Adversarial	Involvement
	Interconnected
Flow of goods	Flow of information
Affluence	Communications
Materiality	Influence
	Knowledge
	Taste
National markets	Global markets
Regionalism	Multinationals
Protectionism	Trade
Local markets	World competition
	World networks
Consumption	Conservation
Immediate gratification	Society
Expansion	Limits
More	Conserve
Stimulating demands	Future resources
	Downsize
	Recycle

Table 9-2 continued

From	*To*
Industrial Economy	*Information Economy*
Centralization	Decentralization
Concentration	Close to markets
Fixed assets	Efficiency
	Commitment
Smokestack industries	High-tech
Specialists	Information rich
Low productivity	Productive
High wages	Generalist
Waste	Adaptive
Pollution	Fixed costs
Information poor	
Power driven	Education driven
Mechanical machines	Universities
Laborers	Computers and electronics
	R&D
	Management skills
Individual entities	Systems
Component efficiency	Total efficiency
Unit objectives	System objectives
Industrialization	Reindustrialization
Mechanization	Government role
Individual initiative	Fair trade
Free trade	Balance of trade
Exports	

Note: see Hawken, p. 79.

just to manufacturing procedures. The information economy will focus on the development of consumption utility by creating user-friendly products and procedures, emphasizing quality, service, and zero defects, and adjusting production and delivery systems to consumer desires. This will reflect a market orientation.

The mass orientation of an industrial economy, mass production, mass distribution and mass consumption will shift to an economy that emphasizes differentiation, customization, individualization, segmenting markets, and developing more flexible production.

The growth philosophy of continuing expansion, and the development of large-scale horizontally and vertically integrated chains is being tempered and replaced. The new orientation emphasizes conservation, contraction, divestiture, and the acceptance of smaller-sized organizations, as is characterized by the slogan "small is beautiful."

In an industrial economy the objective is to accumulate, amass resources, dominate others sometimes, even adopt an adversarial posture. That of the information economy places a greater emphasis on sharing, the mutuality of interests, interconnectedness, and involvement.

Although the industrial economy focuses on the flow of goods, affluence, and materialism, the information economy assumes that they will exist and pays more attention to the flow of information, communications, influence, knowledge, and the development and uplifting of tastes. As markets truly become global with competition among multinational corporations whose plans and decisions transcend local, national, and regional boundaries, they do not merely advance the goals of one country. The age of the true multinational corporation emerges.

The consumption ethic, which is rooted in immediate gratification, getting more, expansion, stimulating demand, and having things now, needs to be modified by a conservation approach. Conservation considers society and its wants, needs, and resources from a long-term perspective, from the perspective of the needs of future generations.

The previous tendency to centralize with large concentrations of fixed assets is replaced by an emphasis on decentralization, getting closer to markets, generating efficiency and gaining commitment from all the organization. And the approaches of the smokestack industries with high wages, low productivity, waste, pollution, a lack of information, and layers of specialists are altered by more emphasis on information-rich, productive, and adaptive systems, with lower fixed costs.

The industrial economy was power driven by both human labor and machines, but the information economy tends to be education driven. It emphasizes the research outputs of universities, R&D activities, computers, electronics, and management skills.

The industrial economy adopted the approach of maximizing individual components, making parts of the system more productive. The information economy seeks to maximize overall efficiency and adopts a systems perspective. There is a movement from industrialization to reindustrialization, mechanization to automation, individual initiative to a prominent role for government, from free trade to fair trade, and unbalanced to balanced trade accounts.

These shifts are not merely extensions of the past but represent breaks from them and changes in orders of magnitude. They make a tremendous difference in corporate operations, management perspectives, and marketplace behavior. They are reshaping and restructuring factors that will affect markets. They shape the marketplace and actions of new consumers.

Consumer Orientations

The new consumers as compared with the more traditional consumers exhibit differences in their orientations as is summarized in table 9–3.

Table 9–3
Changing Consumer Orientations

Traditional Consumers	*New-Breed Consumers*
Materialism	Quality of life
Wife at home	Working wife
Husband–wife duties	Roles blurring
Frugal and save	Spend and enjoy
Make a living	Self-fullfillment
Continuing growth	Limits to growth
Nation-oriented	World-oriented
Sheltered	Exposed/worldly-wise
Acquiescent	Demanding/discerning
Insecure	Sure/confident
Take care of self	Social security
Passive	Active participant
Plebeian tastes	Cosmopolitan

Traditional consumers are more materialistically inclined and emphasize the amassing of products. This is understandable, given the past economic difficulties they encountered, such as the Great Depression. But for the new consumers who have considerable material wealth, it is not merely a matter of more being better, and of accumulation, but of an emphasis on quality of life, and on such quality factors as durability, aesthetics, and reliability of products.

Previously, the majority of wives remained at home with their roles prescribed as taking care of their families. It was working wives who had to justify their situations, with a working wife signaling a husband who could not fulfill his family responsibilities as a provider. Now it is just the reverse because over half the wives are working. This has resulted in major changes in home life, feeding, shopping, entertaining, travel, and childrearing activities. As the majority of wives share both household and breadwinning activities, they work 65–70 hours a week at home and on the job.

In the past, our orientation was one of frugality, saving for a rainy day, buying things when people could afford them, and paying for them in cash. That has been replaced by an orientation of buy now and pay later. Credit purchases are the rule of the day. Plastic has replaced cash so that consumers can spend their future earnings and enhance current enjoyment. And the slogan "enjoy yourself, you only live once" most aptly describes the times.

The work and job perspective has shifted from that of making a living and living to work, with the workplace forming a major, if not *the* major, focus of life. Jobs are now seen as a matter of self-fulfillment and realizing oneself, and not just as a way of earning a living. The basic orientation has become work to live, rather than the previous one of live to work. Other priorities such as family, quality, and style of living are becoming more important than work. The result is that job promotions, particularly those involving relocation and family disruptions, are now assessed far differently than they were in the past and are sometimes even refused.

Consumers are now world oriented for they have a global perspective. They are better traveled and informed and have been exposed to international products and life-styles. This contrasts with the local and regional orientations of more traditional consumers.

As a result, the new consumers now bring the products and life-styles of the world into their homes and surroundings.

The previous expectation of continuous and never-ending growth, emulating the high rates of growth of the 1960s, has been tempered by a recognition of practical limits to growth and the necessity of temporizing actions. This was heightened by the environmental movement and energy crunch of the 1970s, which resulted in greater attention to conservation, pollution, downsizing, recycling, resource efficiency, and environmental monitoring.

Traditional consumers have tended to be more sheltered, less exposed and rather insecure, particularly in their dealings with the business world. The new breed of consumers, being more exposed, better informed, and worldly-wise, have a feeling of greater security. They are surer and more confident of themselves and have become more discerning consumers who demand their rights.

Whereas traditional consumers were more oriented to take care of themselves and their families emphasizing self-reliance and individual responsibility, today consumers are more vocal about the assistance expected from society or the government. Some of the "privileges" of the past, such as jobs, education, and health care are now taking on the mantle of "consumer rights." The new breed of consumers expects government to be supportive of their needs and requests—if not, they will vote a new government into power.

Traditionally, observers and researchers characterized middle-class U.S. consumers as having rather plebian tastes and being culturally unaware. A common reference to the tastes of the middle class was that "all their taste is in the mouth." Bigger was deemed better and that which cost the most money was assessed to be superior.

The new breed of consumers, however, is much better educated, more informed, more aesthetically and culturally aware, and more cosmopolitan in their tastes. Products reflecting good design, aesthetics, taste, color coordination, and graceful life-styles are receiving better acceptance. We are witnessing the dawn of the "cosmopolites"—an increasing mass of consumers with cosmopolitan tastes.

Consumers in the past tended to be more secretive and withdrawn, more reserved, careful of what they said and quite concerned with what the neighbors think. The new consumers are far more open, willing to express themselves and their feelings. They are more concerned with self, taking care of number one. They do not hesitate to express their likes and dislikes.

The traditional consumer was relatively uninformed and automatically accepted authority. The new breed of consumer is better educated, informed, and alert, partly as a result of our improved communications systems. They challenge, question, and seek new ways.

Previously, consumers thought about such privileges as the privilege of receiving an education, having a job, getting enough food, and owning a home. The new breed of consumer thinks of rights—the right to an education, a job, a home, and medical care, the right to be heard, and the right to share in economic prosperity.

Behavioral Determinants

The behavioral determinants refer to those factors that directly influence purchase behavior such as education or mobility. Some of them are product specific, being important to certain products only. Others are more general in nature, and pertain to purchasing behavior overall or to large groups of products. We shall concentrate on them.

Of course, behavioral determinants change through time so that the factors now influencing the purchasing behavior of young marrieds or senior citizens are much different than those of the 1920s or 1930s. The following list presents some of the major behavioral determinants shaping purchase decisions of the new consumer.

No major war

No extended depression

Best educated

Most affluent

Working wives

More first-order births

Smaller-sized families

Travel

Older population

Live longer and healthier

Cultured

Higher expectations

Information-seeking

Leisure-oriented

Mobile

Restless and seek change

Unlike their predecessors the new consumers have not been subjected to an extended major war or to a major depression, two devastating influences. They are the best educated and most affluent, by far, of any consumer group in our history. They have a higher proportion of working wives, with over 52 percent of them in the labor force, one of the most important behavioral influences of all. They have more first births because almost 40 percent of the births are now first born versus the traditional 25 percent. Families are smaller.

Consumers, overall, have much longer life expectancy than they did at the turn of the century. As was noted, the fastest growing age group are those 85 and over; consumers who reach 65 average another 14 years of life. They are healthier and far more exposed to a broad variety of activities.

The new consumers are information-seeking, they are exposed to the world as a result of travel, television, radio, other communications, and are very mobile and leisure-oriented. They are much better informed and worldly-wise.

As a result of different behavioral determinants the outlook and expectations of new-breed consumers are different than those of their parents. Their expectations are that they will be better off than their parents were, that they will enjoy increasing affluence and that the future will be better than the past.

But observers are questioning whether the American Dream of increasing affluence is now being shattered. Average household income in the 1980s has failed to grow and for many of our citizens, low-paying jobs in the lower-paying services sector are replacing those in the higher-paying manufacturing industries. Some workers are currently struggling to maintain their present living standards, to keep from feeling the impact of downward mobility. And should the majority of consumers, or a substantial proportion of them, have to cut back, then social, political and economic consequences would follow.

Yet, regardless of any expressed pessimism about near-term economic conditions, the new consumers basically seem to expect the future to be better for them and their children than are present conditions. They are basically optimistic, assuming that business and government will deliver the good life-style to which they feel entitled (*New York Times* 1986). They are restless, seek change and continuous improvement—they are looking for that which is new. They provide great market opportunities for new products and services.

Summary

A new breed of consumer has appeared in the U.S. marketplace, and differs markedly from consumers of the past three decades. Changing societal and economic forces, as well as new behavioral determinants and consumer orientations, have fashioned the new consumer.

Among the major societal shifts are development of an information rather than an industrial society, an emphasis on decentralized bottom-up management that pays attention to human aspects; the use of flexible, adaptable, automated production systems of appropriate scale and not just of great size; the appearance of participative rather than representative democracy with a focus on outside boards of directors, community interest, and issue politics; the trend to worldism and global rather than national suppliers and markets, with emphasis on abundance as well as boundaries.

The economic shifts focus on the major transitions from an industrial to an information society and the concomitant changes affecting marketing and consumers. Included are an orientation to the creation of user-friendly, quality products that better serve consumer needs and create consumption utility; a greater emphasis on product differentiation, the identification of market segments, and the creation of customized products; a focus on conservation with the tendency to divestiture, contraction, and smaller scale; greater attention to sharing and mutuality of interest of business stakeholders; enhanced flow of information and communications; attention to global consumers, world trade, and international competition; a shift from consumption to conservation, recognizing the limits to resources and future needs; greater decentralization to get closer to consumers; the emergence of high-tech industries, products, and opportunities; our education-driven economy with its needs; the adoption of a systems perspective, and the need for reindustrialization to create jobs and prosperity.

The consumers' new orientation stems from such changes as attention to the quality of life; the increase in working wives with the blurring of husband–wife duties; the orientation to spending, enjoying life, and striving for self-fulfillment on the job; being world-oriented in product choices and becoming more exposed, worldly-wise and cosmopolitan in tastes; recognizing that limits do exist to our prosperity; the development of more demanding, discerning, sure and confident consumers; being active participants in the socioeconomic system and demanding of government support; better-educated, alert, open, and honest consumers; concerned with self rather than others, willing to challenge and question and emphasizing rights, not privileges.

The changing behavioral determinants directly influence purchasing behavior. Included are such new-breed consumer influences as no major war or extended depression; the best-educated and most affluent consumers ever; working wives as a majority; smaller-sized families with a higher proportion of firstborns; an older population that is healthier, cultured, leisure oriented, mobile, and well traveled; consumers who are information-seeking with immediate access to data and who have increasing expectations.

Business strategies, plans, and decisions, based on more traditional consumers, the influences of broad environments, and the economy of the past will be badly out of synch with future markets. The radical shifts occurring require much different business approaches. The challenge confronting business is to harness the market opportunities inherent in the wants and needs of those new consumers and to translate them into profitable products and services.

References

Hawken, Paul. 1983. *The Next Economy.* New York: Holt, Rinehart and Winston.

New York Times. 1986. "New Study Looks at the State of Nation's Old-Age Citizens" (5 August):31.

Index

About the Author

William Lazer is an internationally recognized marketing authority and a consultant to leading U.S. business corporations, governments, and professional associations. He has taught at the University of Manitoba, Michigan State University, and the University of Louvain and has lectured worldwide. Currently he is Eminent Scholar in Business Administration and holder of the Eugene and Christine Lynn Chair at Flordia Atlantic University.

He is the author of numerous books and scores of articles covering a broad spectrum of marketing and management topics, with a particular interest in emerging demographic trends. He has served as the chairman for the Census Advisory Committee (Marketing), past president as well as vice president of the Education and Global Marketing divisions of the American Marketing Association. His honors include: Honorary Doctor of Laws, University of Manitoba; Post Doctoral Ford Foundation fellow, Harvard University; Fellow of the Royal Society of Arts; Beta Gamma Sigma Distinguished Scholar; National Science Foundation Visiting Scholar; Distinguished Faculty Award, Michigan State University. Dr. Lazer was a member of the Blue Ribbon Committee on Trade Negotiations under two U.S. presidents.